UFO⁵ OVER LONG ISLAND, NEW YORK

UFO^s

OVER LONG ISLAND, NEW YORK

JOSEPH FLAMMER

OF THE PARANORMAL ADVENTURERS

Schiffer
Publishing Ltd

4880 Lower Valley Road • Atglen, PA 19310

Dedication

This book is dedicated to all people who have been enduring uninvited alien contact, more than likely their whole lives. I wish I had comfort to offer. I can only advise to fight back! Resist!

As best you can.

Type set in Clicker, Lucida Grande & Georgia

ISBN: 978-0-7643-4707-8
Printed in The United States

Schiffer Books are available at special discounts for bulk purchases for sales promotions or premiums. Special editions, including personalized covers, corporate imprints, and excerpts can be created in large quantities for special needs. For more information contact the publisher:

Published by Schiffer Publishing, Ltd.
4880 Lower Valley Road
Atglen, PA 19310
Phone: (610) 593-1777; Fax: (610) 593-2002
E-mail: Info@schifferbooks.com

For the largest selection of fine reference books on this and related subjects, please visit our website at www.schifferbooks.com.

We are always looking for people to write books on new and related subjects. If you have an idea for a book, please contact us at proposals@schifferbooks.com.

This book may be purchased from the publisher. Please try your bookstore first. You may write for a free catalog.

Acknowledgments

Much thanks to fellow members of the Mutual UFO Network (MUFON) and the diligent UFO trackers of the UFO Reporting Center for their able stewardship of reports of UFOs over Long Island, upon which I relied in this book.

Also thanks to John Ford for receiving me and my partner, Diane Hill, gracefully within the austere confines of the upstate prison hospital where he has been incarcerated for over 17 years. Ford was arrested, put away, and silenced for alleged crimes related to his warnings to Long Islanders about the silent UFO invasion of Long Island.

Also thanks to Diane Hill, my investigations partner, who experienced with me many of the unbelievable events about to be revealed in the pages of this book.

Finally, thanks to all the people who contributed their knowledge, stories, and photographs to this book, with a particular thanks to movie-maker Daniel Marquardt of Bay Shore, who allowed me to publish his photos of a light anomaly in the sky over Jones Beach.

CONTENTS

PART II

Chapter Four: 2013:
Alien Telepathic Trickery? . . . 45

Chapter Five:
Anti-UFO Army Helicopters
Visit Rocky Point . . . 51

Chapter Six:
2010: Long Island Devil
Investigation Revisited . . . 63

PART III

Chapter Seven:
UFOs Over the Pine Barrens . . . 75

PART IV

Chapter Eight:
The Continuous Search For Answers . . . 113

PART V

Chapter Nine:
Calling All Extraterrestrials . . . 134

PART VI

Conclusion . . . 151

UFO captured at dusk by Daniel Marquardt of Bay Shore, while filming the sunset over Jones Beach for a tourism documentary he was producing for his company, SawGrass Productions. He said a red object, like a laser beam, was emitted from the larger blue object. Mr. Marquardt said the silent UFO hovered over the Robert Moses Bridge. He took seventeen photos of it as it moved around the sky before he switched to video. The video is posted on YouTube: http://www.youtube.com/watch?v=QtUju9m-qBU.

THE GREAT NEW YORK BLACKOUT OF 1965

The Long Island sky was a cool, dusky blue that fateful late afternoon. The time was just about 5:20 p.m. The date was November 9, 1965. It would be remembered as the day of the Great New York Blackout.

The blackout was a calamity of great proportions. Many people at the time believed it was caused by extraterrestrials in spaceships. UFOs and luminous orbs were seen across New York State and elsewhere that very afternoon.

To the believers who saw the crafts, the associated blackout was an event that signaled the beginning of a time when alien beings felt free to tamper with human infrastructure—possibly to learn how it works, possibly to recharge their spaceship batteries with our electricity, or possibly for some darker reason that we may never know.

The year 1965 was also about the same time people started reporting abductions of humans by aliens. Barney and Betty Hill, for example, were a church-going couple who claimed to have been abducted while driving in the dark of night somewhere around the Old Man on the Mountain in Franconia Notch, New Hampshire, in 1961. Their story came out in 1965.

The Hills claimed they were examined with probes and shown a map of stars. They remembered many details later while under hypnosis. The map that their alien abductors showed them was said to show the star system that was home to the space visitors. Thus, if we can believe the abduction stories, space creatures during this time were not only tampering with human infrastructure, like the electric power supplying a large piece of the United States, but they were also interfering in human lives, stealing people against their wills as they drove along a country highway in the White Mountains. For all we know, the aliens might have been interfering in human history for millennia.

What we do know for sure is that, in 1965, our infrastructure wasn't theirs to experiment with—nor will it ever be—and our lives will never be theirs to abduct. Our bodies are not theirs to bring to spaceship laboratories to penetrate with anal probes and silvery eyeball and navel needles. This planet belongs to us: human beings.

While it is true that we humans are of the Earth, we are strangely also above it. We are superior in intellect to all other creatures that inhabit our planet. Some theorists believe aliens tampered with our genes long ago to develop a race of superior primates. For sure, we humans are somewhat disconnected from the hardship other animals seem to suffer because of the amazing technology we have developed, starting with the use of fire and the invention of tools. From there, we flew as a species. We are the only species on the planet to have produced Shakespeare, Beethoven, Einstein, and the Beatles. Life forms from other solar systems, galaxies, or even universes have no right to abduct anyone on planet Earth for their own purposes. We are a species to be reckoned with.

The enormous power outage the day of the blackout was eventually blamed on a faulty relay on the Canadian side of Niagara Falls. It triggered a power surge that roared down through Vermont, New Hampshire, Massachusetts, Rhode Island, Connecticut, New York, and New Jersey. Like being struck by a lightning bolt, power stations tripped offline all down through the Northeastern United States. Practically a third of the population of the United States was without power. It left people in the dark in an area covering over 80,000 square miles. Some folks didn't get power back until thirteen hours later.

The *New York Times* reported 80,000 people were stranded in the New York City subway system because the blackout struck at the height of rush hour. Over 30 million people in all would find themselves without electricity. Lights went dead. Traffic became a mess. Airplanes couldn't land.

But the Great New York Blackout didn't hit Long Island just then. It would strike like a cobra in about five minutes. I was one of the people who saw something in the sky just before the cobra bit Long Island.

★

"Go ahead; just jump!" Weston said to me with another bullying glance.

He wiped his leaky nose with the dirty end of his gray sweatshirt and snorted back another slick of snot, cautiously peeking over the edge of the barn's black roof down at the hard ground below. It was a big jump. It would be a hard landing, especially while only wearing sneakers.

"Why should I jump? You're the one who said you were going to do it, not me!" I yelled back.

We were both standing on the sharp decline of old Mr. Terrell's big, red, broken barn on the small farm he operated on Anchor Avenue in Oceanside, Long Island. I was nine years old.

Weston snorted back another liquid line dripping down from his nostrils and glanced to the rooftops of the houses around us. We were eye level with some of the roofs, higher up than many of the kitchen roofs in the neighborhood. We saw a lot of sky.

Weston was a big boy—bigger than me—and he had a tendency towards violence. He was strong and intimidating. When boys refused to do what he wanted, he threw them fierce unreadable glances that always threatened a hard whack to the stomach or thud punch to the chest when least expected.

"Just jump," he bullied once again, and then looked over the edge down at the long, scary drop. I could tell by the way he jerked his head back that his stomach tingled just like mine when he looked down.

"*You* jump; I'm not doing it!" I shouted, and I sat down on the tired, black shingles, careful not to lose my balance. Sliding off this roof to the ground—ten or twelve feet below—would surely mean a broken ankle or leg. I wanted to get home to a spaghetti and hot bread dinner that should be ready soon; I didn't want to go to the hospital in pain.

Weston dropped to his hams, too. He was not about to jump. He was giving up trying to get me to, as well. His mouth was forming to utter a threatening rebuke when suddenly a ferocious roar came out of the southern sky.

The scream of a thunderous projectile sounded like a trumpet from the area south of us, from out of the nearby Atlantic Ocean, where we often swam and fished. We turned our heads in a flash to that portion of the sky that faced Long Beach. At that instant, we witnessed a red fireball the size of a school building flying over the houses of our town and over us and onward north, all in a second, without smoke, without our comprehension.

We stood up, and without speaking, followed the smokeless fireball on its journey towards the mountains of upstate New York and beyond towards distant Canada.

Instinctively, we rushed to the dingy, white pipe at the side of the barn and slid down to the wood boxes we had set up and carefully dropped down the rest of the way to the ground. We still hadn't said a word. We flew beside each other on our Stingray bicycles, banana seats with STP stickers on them, Yankees baseball cards clamped on the spokes and clicking as the wheels turned, down the block to the big area of sky near the church on the spacious corner. We stopped and searched the wide, darkening vista to see if there was any sign of anything else coming. Would the thing that was on fire come back?

"What *was* that?" Weston asked as his frightened brown eyes searched the ash-blue sky.

"I think it was a spaceship on fire," I said. "I saw it was round. I saw fire."

"And something like a room was on top, right?" he asked pleadingly. He looked to my eyes. He was gauging whether or not I saw the dome on the top of the burning craft.

"I saw it, too, yes," I said. "It looked like a bubble."

"Yeah," he said, "a bubble," and we immediately parted company. We would fly home to tell our mothers what we saw.

Weston never bothered me again after that. He didn't like to talk to me anymore, either. I think I reminded him of something he was scared of. And we never spoke of the burning spaceship again. We were both probably too scared much more of the spaceship than jumping off old Mr. Terrell's barn roof.

Two minutes later, New York went dark.

PART I

CHAPTER ONE

THE LONG ISLAND ALIEN NIGHTMARE BEGINS

1

My story begins in 1989.

I was a newspaper reporter back then. Hell, I had been a newspaper reporter for more than half my life by the time all this upside down nightmarish insanity started with animal mutilations and spaceships crashing in local parks and whatnot. I was in my early thirties. I'm in my fifties now. I guess I'm an old geezer, but I don't feel like one.

For me, the reality of the silent alien invasion of Long Island really started with dead animals: livestock mutilated in the middle of the summer night on a windblown East End farm. I wrote newspaper stories about dead bullfrogs floating upside down at a county park (see section 43). The lady who called me about discovering the bullfrogs held her hand to her mouth as I turned one over at the water's edge to inspect its missing eyes.

At the same time came reports of UFO sightings. Things were happening quickly, as though the UFOs were accelerating over Long Island. I listened carefully to the people I interviewed. Their experiences always brought my mind back to the fireball burning across the darkening sky on November 9, 1965, the day of the Great New York Blackout. Except I knew what I saw wasn't just a fireball. It was much more. It was a UFO. It was one just like some of the UFOs people were talking about. Because of what I saw that day, I understood the strangeness of the things people said, though the particulars of the things they called "UFOs" varied.

The reports I was hearing in 1989, of flying vehicles were that they were cigar-shaped, disk-shaped, and triangular-shaped spaceships. These reports were witnessed by credible people. Many of the Long Islanders with whom I spoke were embarrassed to even tell me their stories. These were people who were competent at life, not mentally ill. They held steady jobs, had children, spouses, pets, and licenses.

The incomprehensible machines people were observing hovered over Long Island's sparkling blue bays at dusk. They were spotted flying over the black waters of the Atlantic Ocean at night. They were seen hovering near steely railroad tracks in Port Jefferson, over garages in West Hempstead, and in backyards in the wilds of verdant Manorville.

2

Interviews continue.

In more recent years, such as 2011, 2012, and 2013, I would resume my interviews with people who claimed to see spaceships over Long Island. The new interviews continued a seemingly unbroken chain of UFO sightings over the region. In resurrecting my studies of UFOs, I felt like I had never taken a twenty-year break. I suddenly started hearing, once again, the same kind of stories I had grown so familiar hearing in 1989 and in neighboring years. The sightings simply stretched into the future, as if nothing at all had changed, as if neither the government nor anyone else had solved the problem of aliens invading Long Island.

What else can you call it but an "invasion"? How do you describe the introduction of an alien race or races to Long Island other than calling it an invasion?

In 2012, I would interview Laura Hendrickson of Cutchogue. In her 50s, Laura is an instructor of developmentally disabled adults, and a skeptic of anything paranormal. She explained that she never had an interest in UFOs before her own experience in a rural area of eastern Long Island only months earlier.

> "I was driving alone on North Road in Cutchogue last year," Ms. Hendrickson began, "when I saw a UFO in the sky." She looked up at the ceiling in the room where we were sitting as if seeing the spaceship all over again. "Whatever this thing was, it was big—I mean big! It was just stationary in the sky." She looked down at me. "The object was dark and shaped like a triangle. It just stayed there. Nobody else was on the road at that time. I was all alone. I just watched it. Then, all at once, it shot off and was gone! Where was it from?" She paused. "I have no idea."

Paranormal researcher Mike Salvia atop the Fire Island Lighthouse during a paranormal investigation.

Michael Salvia, a noted paranormal investigator in his 40s from Old Bethpage, said he believes aliens could be using Long Island as a rest stop because of its location, stretching as it does into the depths of the cold Atlantic. "I think extraterrestrials are interested in our water, and that's why they're here," he said.

Salvia can quickly summon details of the tremendous spaceship he claims he witnessed over Long Island in 2005.

> "It overtook the sky!" remembered the security guard. "It was black and the size of a couple of football fields. It blocked out the stars."

> Salvia said his wake-up call to the practice of UFOs visiting Long Island came one night when he and a friend witnessed a craft floating high over busy East Meadow, a relatively small Long Island hamlet of only 6.3 square miles with a population of over 38,000.

"It was blacker than black," Salvia recalled. "We could see it blocking out the stars. It was darker than the night sky."

At first Salvia thought the craft was a jet, but he soon realized it was too large to be a jet. Moreover, the spaceship was silently hovering in one spot in the sky.

"Sometimes it would pull a fast maneuver and shoot off, but it would soon return right back to a hovering position," Salvia recalled. It was then he realized he was probably observing an alien craft.

Reminiscent of reports of spaceships seen by thousands of people in the area of Phoenix, Arizona in 1997, Salvia said, "It floated over East Meadow for a long time, and then just disappeared. A lot of people saw it. A girl I knew in Westbury, a town far away from East Meadow, told me she saw the same thing that night. She told this to me before I had even mentioned my sighting to her, so it's not like I fed her any information."

Daniel Marquardt of Bay Shore, on the other hand, expressed great uneasiness at labeling the object he saw and photographed in the sky over Jones Beach in 2011 a "UFO." He expressed discomfort with the way people negatively view witnesses who report seeing alleged unidentified flying objects in the sky.

"I'm not going to call what I saw in the sky a UFO," he began. "I think of myself as one of the sanest people I know. I don't know what it was, but it hovered over the Robert Moses Bridge and something like a red laser beam came out of it."

Marquardt, the president and founder of SawGrass Productions, Inc., said he was on the Wantagh Parkway, filming a time-lapsed movie of the sunset over Jones Beach for a tourism documentary he was creating, when he saw a blue object fly out of dark clouds. Using his cell phone, he was able to shoot seventeen photos of the object and also caught it with the phone's video application.

3

The Nightmare for Long Islanders.

With the coming of the spaceships in 1989, a nightmare for me and other Long Islanders began that I hope one day we can somehow manage to turn into a positive for all people—but I doubt I'll ever see that happen, nor will you in your lifetime, most probably, dear reader. Nonetheless, it's my hope that one day humans will establish a dialogue with our alien invaders and gain knowledge of advanced technologies from them that will improve the lives of all humans by fighting diseases, creating safe, clean energy, and reducing pollution to the ozone layer. But mostly, I hope the aliens inadvertently teach us how to get rid of them. They don't belong on this planet. Thousands of generations of their ancestors didn't work and suffer to exist on this planet as ours did.

But even with all the evidence piled up before me in 1989—such as eye witnesses telling me their stories of sightings and abductions by aliens, and of animal mutilations on an East End farm, and after turning over dead bullfrogs without eyes in a pond in a county park, and even having seen the thunderous fireball with a bubble on top on the day of the Great New York Blackout of 1965—the evidence piled up before me was not nearly enough to convince me that UFOs were real, and that they were really over Long Island.

For me, the convincing evidence that we are being visited came in 2013, in the form of a huge spaceship hovering over Garden City. We'll get to that incident soon enough.

CHAPTER TWO

THE LONG ISLAND DEVIL

Extraterrestrial, Ghost, or Ghoul?

4

No time to waste.

Artist's conception of The Long Island Devil. *Drawing by Karen Isaksen.*

You must understand, there wasn't any time to waste.

The need for a paranormal investigation was immediate. Emergency! Code Red! Sound the alarms!

I gazed out the window of my home office into the yellow afternoon sunlight. Rays of honey-light bronzed the bare winter trees in my big yard.

It was mid-March on Long Island, 2010. The familiar maple and oak trees, bending ever more earnestly towards the promise of warm spring, would soon be budding. The deer living in the Rocky Point Preserve in the Pine Barrens, a mile away from my house, would be birthing. Bicyclists wearing colorful skin-tight outfits would soon be riding up and down the local country roads in large groups as they do every spring. Emerging blades of grass in disorderly clumps in my yard would need to be mowed once again. I'd have to tune up the cantankerous red lawn mower. I'd need to rake up a ton of crisp brown leaves and fallen twigs, branches, and thick tree limbs that fell during forgotten storms over the winter.

But household tasks would have to be put on the back burner for the time being. Something far more urgent was calling. The Long Island Devil was out there. Finding the creature couldn't wait.

Spring was right around the corner. Spring would be the time to start this investigation. It would be a special investigation, the only one of its kind ever to occur on Long Island. It couldn't wait till summer.

There were just a few short weeks to get this investigation up and running or the opportunity would just blow by. I had to catch investigators who I needed to help me on this quest before they went on summer vacation. I needed them on Long Island and I needed to start organizing them into a group of investigators right now!

All this meant I had to get the work of creating a plan and making phone calls done now, too, before summer set in. I needed a good team of investigators to work with me in solving one of the greatest mysteries on Long Island—the Case of the Long Island Devil.

Nobody knew what the creature was. Was it a monster, a Bigfoot, a ghost, an inter-dimensional being, a ghoul, an angel, a Guardian, a demon, or something else? If investigators should be away on vacation, then solving the cryptozoological puzzle of what the creature of Farmingdale really was could be squandered. The Devil might move on. It would make the job of finding the beast impossible.

Meanwhile, there was my regular job to contend with. Damn! I'd have to switch some things around and change my work schedule.

And then there was our lecturing; Diane Hill and I had a slew of lectures about ghosts and the paranormal slated for libraries in the spring. We had been speaking at about sixty libraries a year for seven years. The dates were already booked. I'd have to plan a schedule for the investigators that could work around those days.

"Where am I going to find the time for this investigation?" I wondered as I gazed out the window at the trees. I paused before I thought aloud: "I have to *make* the time. It's that important."

I only hoped this thing, this alleged monster, the reported black graveyard ghoul of Farmingdale described by a witness as possibly part human and part something else—indeed—would still be hiding in the local woods when my team and I got around to searching for it.

I daydreamed through the slits of the wooden blinds in my old room in my old house in the old hills of Rocky Point. *Should I call the police or the National Guard to report what I know about this creature?* I wondered. *What would I say? That a monster was loose on Long Island? That a black creature fell from a spaceship and is now roaming around the woods of Farmingdale and Bethpage without anyone trying to find out what it was?*

I had to put an investigative team together right away. It was my responsibility. I knew what I had to do. A six-foot tall, charcoal black, humanoid monster that can fly, has two legs and two arms, two wings, wears a cape and a hood, and can disappear at will sounds mighty dangerous to me. That the entity allegedly lives in or around a group of small graveyards scared me even more. According to stories from around the world, it's in graveyards where ghouls dwell. Ghouls, according to Arabic folklore, eat children. Similar creatures to the Long Island Devil have been seen around the world. Sometimes they accost children, like young girls, the dreadful stories claimed.

I read through the names of people who signed our black and white marble notebook at recent library lectures. These were people who wanted to be contacted to participate in an investigation with Diane and me, if one should arise. I was sure these people would understand my concern about this alleged beast. By the yellow sunlight, I marked the first thirty names in the signup book. They were names gotten from our most recent visits to the Farmingdale and Bethpage Public Libraries, where Diane Hill and I recently spoke about ghosts as *The Paranormal Adventurers*. Bethpage and Farmingdale are neighboring hamlets, the very places where all this monster activity was allegedly happening.

The names I marked on the pages of the notebook belonged to people who signed up to go out with Diane and me on an investigation the next time we should schedule such an open, free event. We held these types of public ghost hunts for our audience members from time to time, and they were always hugely successful. That's thanks to ghost-hunting friends who have helped us keep it all together. Sometimes these investigations drew fifty or more people. The gatherings were great fun. Diane and I forged some lasting relationships with fellow Long Islanders on these outings. We also got to know some extraordinary ghost investigators who have taught us a lot over the years.

In the margins of the page in the notebook, I wrote the names of a handful of experienced Long Island paranormal investigators I wanted to join us. These included Peggy Vetrano and William Sanchez of *Eastern Suffolk Paranormal* (ESP), because they think outside the box and effectively challenge the spirits to present themselves in one way or another. I wrote the names of Kevin Kelly,

Bill Berongi, and Keith Baecker of *Long Island Paranormal Seekers*. They are organized and brave, and they have stories to tell about Sweet Hollow Road and other places that would curl your toes back. I wrote the names of Mark and David Koenigsmann; they are a father-and-son team from Massapequa Park who consistently get results that astound fellow ghost hunters. It was the Koenigsmann team who saw a little girl in colonial garb walking across Potter's Field Cemetery at night during a ghost hunt.

I also wrote in the margin the names of about six other top field investigators who I liked because they could lead the newer investigators and keep the latches buttoned down, you might say. Don't get me wrong, the newer investigators were just as important and valuable as the more experienced hunters. It's just that the lead investigators I picked were experienced people who could help run the show and keep everyone together on the same page. This included advising the others about the safety issues associated with graveyards at night and the dangers of being confronted suddenly by ghosts. Ghosts can be so frightening that they have turned people's hair white on the spot. These lead investigators knew how to manage newcomers to optimize success. A successful ghost hunt is one in which everyone remains safe, yet experiences the "sleight-of-hand" of the paranormal. Perhaps one might hear or feel the spirits or even see ghosts. The lead investigators I chose knew what paranormal signs to look for and how to keep the spirits communicating. They could teach neophytes the ropes through example.

I looked down at the names of the people who said they wanted to go ghost hunting with us. I didn't know most of them, because the only time I ever met them was when they attended a lecture Diane and I were giving.

Well, guess what folks, this is it! I thought. *Now is the time I need you!* I turned to the computer and started writing e-mails to these volunteers.

The historic investigation that would result would come to be known as the Long Island Devil Investigation. It was the largest paranormal investigation ever to be conducted on Long Island.

CHAPTER THREE

CE-5
Calling UFOs to Earth

5

A frigid winter night.

Almshouse Cemetery in Yaphank. This is where the Long Island CE-5 Group met at night.

Donned in boots, gloves, and other heavy winter clothing, we seven hearty students of the Unknown trudged through the small gravestones in the dark and creepy cemetery under a black March night sky in search of UFOs. Three years earlier, in 2010, I had done this with over forty other investigators in the graveyards of Farmingdale, looking for the Long Island Devil—with no success.

But tonight was not about the Long Island Devil. We had gathered together on this frigid night in Almshouse Cemetery, better known as Potter's Field Cemetery, to make direct contact with extraterrestrials.

Almshouse Cemetery is a little-known graveyard in the rural Pine Barrens of Yaphank. Believe it or not, the seven of us were here to look up at the blazing stars and call alien spaceships down to Earth so we could meet beings from other planets face-to-face.

Most of us didn't know each other because it was the first time we had ever assembled as a group. Before tonight we were just names and pictures interfacing on the Internet in a CE-5 (Close Encounters of the 5th Kind) meet up group.

Almshouse Cemetery is known to ghost researchers as a well-established, haunted graveyard. Ghosts reside here. As mentioned, this is where the Koenigsmann father-and-son team saw the little girl in colonial garb walk across the graveyard only to disappear. It's located right next to the Exit 67 entrance ramp going east on the Long Island Expressway. A thousand souls who once lived and died in the old Suffolk County Poorhouse were buried in this graveyard—not by name, but by numbers etched into the faces of their tiny impersonal gravestones. It's a dark place at night, and that was why we picked it as our site to look up into the heavens to search for alien crafts, and then call them down to visit us on Earth.

The graveyard can be found just a handful of miles north through the woods from infamous Southaven Park. That's the large Suffolk County park where a small silvery spaceship reportedly crashed in 1992. It was believed by some Long Island Ufologists at the time that alien bodies were collected by secretive government agents in black uniforms that bore no insignias. The park was closed for four days following the alleged crash, but park officials said it was closed to accommodate duck hunters, not special government black ops teams cleaning up evidence of an alien invasion (see section 44).

The Long Island UFO Network (LIUFON), a now all but defunct, trailblazing UFO research group, produced an anonymous video that was reportedly shot at the crash site on the notorious night of the alleged UFO crash. The muddled video was later given to a fireman who turned it over to the *South Shore Press* newspaper for review. The *South Shore Press* had a couple good writers and editors working for them at the time; they wrote the story of the event as told to them by LIUFON members. The video, which I have reviewed by looking it up on the Internet [http://www.youtube.com/watch?v=LgtFrfrvcWk] , shows men studying silvery items in an outdoor environment at night.

The UFO researchers of LIUFON were as militant a UFO research club as could possibly be at the time. Militant is not a bad word; it denotes passion, in this case. The researchers claimed alien bodies from the spaceship crash were brought to nearby Brookhaven National Laboratory, a heavily guarded U.S. Department of Energy facility known to Long Islanders as "The Lab." It was a secretive place where military experiments were said to be conducted. The secure site still has its own nuclear power plant. Once there, the aliens underwent autopsies and were prepared for safe keeping, the investigators said.

Some folks have suggested the bodies of the aliens were then sent to Area 51 in Nevada or perhaps to the military base in Florida where President Richard Nixon reportedly brought his good friend, comedian Jackie Gleason, to view

Infamous Southaven Park in Suffolk County. This is the park where a spaceship allegedly crashed and alien bodies were recovered in 1992.

dead alien bodies, but it's impossible to know (see section 45).

Referring to research conducted by LIUFON members in the six months following the supposed crash, the *South Shore Press* published an article about the alleged incident. Though the publication of the article was half a year removed from the supposed crash, the newspaper finally drew the public's attention to LIUFON's outcry about a spaceship breaking apart over Long Island and crashing into the park, and, of course, the subsequent alleged government cover up.

Now here we were tonight, the seven of us, in a known haunted graveyard with only the dark, dank woods of winter separating us from secretive Southaven Park.

Who knew what lurked in the miles of inky woods in between? It was widely known, for example, that often at night, multiple helicopters flew in search patterns for hours over the Pine Barrens for unknown reasons. I witnessed this myself twice in late February and early March 2013. I watched the helicopters from the front porch of a house located smack in the heart of the pine woods (see section 16).

One day, in 2013, I saw and photographed helicopters carrying trucks and other equipment over the woods. Meanwhile, that same day, military Humvees and Jeeps maneuvered through the narrow back roads that crossed the woods. What they were doing amid the trees is anyone's guess. The Rocky Point Preserve, 5,249 acres of woods, is where this particular series of events occurred. The same woods are reserved for New York State residents' recreational use—not military exercises. The soldiers were in the woods on this spring day in 2013 for something that happened deep inside the trees and was never reported by the press. The Anti-UFO Army had mobilized for some unknown reason. Was it another UFO crash like the one at Southaven Park?

It's my firm belief the helicopters I witnessed over the Pine Barrens on many other nights were also military, because they were enormous and their blades ripped the sky apart like gods casting down vengeance upon mankind. The thunderous cutting of the heavy blades was alarming. What were the soldiers looking for? What branch of the military did they belong to?

I was frightened those nights as I stood observing the helicopters' blinding spot lights shining down on the mysterious woods all around me. What were they looking for in the trees? What was it they were reacting to? Was it true that aliens had an interest in the Pine Barrens as some people claimed? Did their spaceships land in the woods as some people said? Were government agents searching for an extraterrestrial base, or lone spaceship, or a survivor alien from the Southaven Park crash that still wandered the woods alone and afraid, trying to find a way home after all these years? Are they looking for the Long Island Devil, the untrackable creature seen in Farmingdale by a variety of people over the years?

6

Bizarre cases.

Witnesses around the world were reporting bizarre cases of alien abductions, missing time, and Men in Black. These incidents were experienced by Long Islanders, too—and by people who'd never had any previous interest in UFOs. Hearing their terrifying stories chilled me. Little did I know back then that I'd be writing a book to tell you that the same things eventually happened to me in 2013, starting with the sighting of an enormous spacecraft over Garden City (see section 15).

Some of the people with whom I spoke would regain consciousness an hour after being abducted. They wouldn't know how they got to the place they ended up. They experienced cases of missing time.

It happened to Tall Al (see section 36). His was the first case of an alien abduction on Long Island that I'd ever heard about. I was just a kid—11 years old. I heard his story two years after I had witnessed the fireball cutting through the sky on the day of the 1965 Blackout.

Tall Al was a thin, lanky man with a long face, pale skin, and a gray, bald head with just a few long strands of useless straw hair combed across it. But most noticeable were his intense, stark-raving mad black eyes that followed you down the street after he told you his upsetting story.

Al lived in an apartment above a store in the town of Oceanside, where I grew up. He was probably 45 years old. I always thought he looked like Ichabod

Crane. His arms were too long and his legs were so lanky that he walked like a camel. I don't think he had a job. He had a little yellow dog that pawed merrily up and down streets with him all around town all the time. Tall Al would tell anybody who'd listen to him about what happened with the spaceship at the creek.

Tall Al's apartment was above a luncheonette that featured a greasy window. The luncheonette was located in the heart of town, across from the blue and white police booth in the small triangle facing the funeral home. His alleged abduction was much like Janet Russell's, though the two cases were completely unrelated, but occurring about the same time. (You're probably not going to believe Janet Russell's story because it involves hybrid humans she saw in glass jars aboard a spacecraft when she was abducted. See section 34.) As you'll learn as you read on, both Tall Al and Janet Russell each lost an hour of time and later came to learn they had been in a spaceship during that time.

Janet Russell is a famous Long Island psychic who had her own pubic access television show, *Beyond the Unknown,* which Diane and I were on twice, talking about Long Island's ghosts. We'll get to her story and more about Tall Al shortly.

7

Back to 2010: The Devil.

The people I contacted to join me on the Long Island Devil Investigation of 2010 were the right people for the job, okay.

In fact, many of the folks who participated in the following three-month investigation fully agreed with a talented psychic in the group, who told us on the last day of the investigation that we were all meant to be part of the search for the Long Island Devil, that we had been invited by the spirits because we, and only we, were meant to uncover secrets that hitherto no one else knew, including the burning at the stake of a Long Island witch. They agreed with the psychic that it was preplanned by greater forces than ourselves that we should all come together. Some of us nodded and said there is no such thing as coincidence.

I called the being that supposedly had been seen in the Bethpage-Farmingdale area The Long Island Devil. I gave it this name because tales of the alleged monster reminded me of the Jersey Devil, a mysterious beast of legends that has reportedly been seen in the Pinelands of New Jersey since 1735. The "Pinelands" are Pine Barrens, just like Long Island's Pine Barrens.

Now, it seemed, the Jersey Devil—or something like it—was on Long Island.

Or, if you believe the story about the Southaven Park UFO crash in the Shirley in 1992, where Ufologists from LIUFON claimed bodies of dead aliens were collected by the government, then this thing that allegedly appeared to people in Farmingdale might have been an extraterrestrial. According to this line of thinking, the creature survived the spaceship crash in Southaven Park, or perhaps another crash, and escaped capture by the government agents in roaring unmarked trucks chasing behind it. It escaped eastern Long Island. Now it roams the woods of central Long Island alone, hiding from authorities who undoubtedly are still after it, if it's an extraterrestrial.

Like the elusive mountain lion I pursued in the Pine Barrens when I was a reporter in 1989, I could not find the Long Island Devil in 2010. Maybe the extraterrestrial hides in the woods, waiting to be saved by its brethren when the mother ship returns. Maybe it's skilled at hiding and disguising itself. One notion is that it takes the shape of a large tree tumor and hugs a tree when in plain sight of humans, masking its body from our perceptions. Maybe we'll never find the creature, if it exists, because of such creative tactics.

Of course, the story of the Long Island Devil sounds ridiculous to most people because it's hard to believe. But so, too, are the stories told to Diane Hill and me of a monster in the woods seen by two female eye-witnesses and reported in *Ghosts, Ghouls, & Monsters of Long Island* (Schiffer Publishing: 2012). These witnesses shared accounts of a red-eyed, black creature they spotted in the trees of Bethpage State Park at night. They claimed it was watching them as they worked at a stable where they taught horseback riding. Diane and I recorded their stories on video. The witnesses believe something non-human watched them on at least one night.

8

In the beginning.

But let me start at the beginning. It's where I know you wanted me to begin in the first place.

Diane and I got wind of this mysterious creature through Patrick Kenney. He's a polite, kindly church worker in his 40s. Patrick is from Farmingdale. He said he first spotted the cryptid, now called the Long Island Devil, high up in a tree near where he lived with his parents in a fine house on a tree-lined residential street in Farmingdale in 2008. It was springtime, and people were eager to be outside for a change of scenery because they had been cooped up all winter. Now that the snow had thawed and the trees were starting to change, people needed to spend more time out-of-doors in the fresh air.

Kenney said the alleged monster was watching a group of these eager people as they enjoyed a springtime picnic behind a fence in a backyard. He said he and his little dog spotted the beast high in the tree while they were taking a daytime stroll. He couldn't really see the people having the picnic in the backyard, he said, because they were behind a fence that blocked his view from the street where he stood with his dog; but he could hear the people partying, talking, and laughing.

The fence may explain why the creature was high up on the limb of a tall tree. The ghoul or extraterrestrial, or ghost, or whatever it was, might have been watching the activities in the backyard from a place high above the fence, where it had an unobstructed view. Perhaps the creature was interested in the food the people were eating.

Patrick said the entity pointed its long, black, bony finger at the people. It paid no attention to him or to his dog. Maybe it smelled the food from the trees in the cluster of small graveyards down the block and flew invisibly through the daylight to see if it could steal a quick bite. I and other investigators would later come to believe that if there really was such a creature out there—and we have reason to believe there really could be—then it probably came from either the graveyards down the block near Patrick's house or from the 1,400 acres of greenery of Bethpage State Park, which is located directly across a narrow road from the graveyards. By the end of the investigation, we would suspect that the entity dwelled in the woods, and sometimes the graveyards—if it was real and dwelled any place.

Moreover, through strips of greenery, the Devil could have access to the enormous area of parklands, including those woods that cover Mount Misery to the north and the mega cemeteries in Farmingdale. Mount Misery is a tall hill that spans about a mile in any direction. It's located in Melville and West Hills. This is an area where people have long claimed seeing a tall creature in a hood and cape with burning red eyes at night. Some people said it was Mothman, the creature described in John A. Keel's 1975 book, *The Mothman Prophecies*. Keel himself talked about UFOs over Mount Misery in the book.

But I'm jumping ahead of myself. Please stay with me. It's easy for me to want to advance too quickly because I want to get to the point.

So, Patrick Kenney and his little dog looked up at the Long Island Devil in as much astonishment as one could imagine. Picture yourself in this case. Think of the things that would be going through your mind if you saw such a creature in a tree in your neighborhood.

Patrick described it to me as all black and in a cape and hood, though he said the hood might have been the top of the creature's wings, cupping the back of its head. It was hard to tell. He said it had long fingers, probably stood six feet tall, and weighed about ninety pounds. He added that the entity disappeared into thin air before his eyes. In all, he and his dog watched it for about two minutes, he said.

Then, *Poof!*

"It turned into particles or something," Kenney explained, at a total loss to make sense of what he had seen.

Let me ask you now, dear reader: Wouldn't you feel it was your responsibility to pursue this creature with earnestness and vigor as soon as you feasibly could, especially if you were the only paranormal investigator who had this information? Wouldn't you be concerned for the safety of people in the neighborhood where Kenney said he saw the beast? Think of all the kids in the area. Remember, ghouls are associated with graveyards and eating children.

I know I would act; and I did.

It all began when Diane and I were lecturing, in 2009, in Farmingdale Public Library as *The Paranormal Adventurers*. That's when soft-spoken Patrick Kenney, a gentleman with silver hair and glasses on his boyish nose, came up to us after the lecture (as many people do) and asked me timidly what I thought the creature he saw in the tree could have been. We had never met before. He explained the sighting to me in a minute or less. He told me what it looked like and how it moved. He did the best he could with other people standing around listening, waiting to talk to me. He had only a brief chance to explain himself. I felt badly for not giving his story more time and consideration. I didn't know what the creature could have been and I told him so. And he left.

But his story fascinated me. I took his phone number at the end of our minute discussion and said I'd call him to look into it further. I called about three months later when Diane and I had a clearing in our lecturing and investigations schedule. Diane came with me to Farmingdale to speak with Patrick. People often think I'm the lead investigator between us. But what they don't know is that Diane does her own homework, her own way, and stays more in the background, sometimes to get a different perspective on a matter. It's not planned that way; it just works out that way. That's one of the reasons we think of ourselves as a good team.

It was a bright weekend day. We met Patrick and a handful of his friends at his home and walked to the nearby site where he said he saw the Devil. It was only a short walk of about two blocks. I recorded about an hour's worth of testimony from Patrick that day, both on video and on a voice recorder. I asked him a lot of the same questions in different ways, trying to punch holes into his story. But I couldn't. His testimony held up to my satisfaction.

According to Patrick, somewhere out there, in the creeping mists of the cold Long Island night, is a lone black creature, a humanoid, or something like one, that lives amongst us without allowing us to know it or it knowing us. Later, we would learn of this creature's connection to the group of old graveyards in Patrick's neighborhood. It is well established in folklore that graveyards are where ghouls emerge at night. Are ghouls real? If you lived in Patrick's neighborhood, would you really want to find out by one appearing in a tree overlooking your yard?

So what was the thing he saw? Was it the Mothman, a graveyard ghoul, or was it an escaped alien from a crashed spaceship?

9

CE-5 Group: 2013.

We six men and one woman, trudging through the Potter's Field graveyard in Yaphank, were the members of a newly formed CE-5 group. I seem to recall that it was the only group of its kind on Long Island at the time, though there were other such clubs formed here and there throughout the United States. Admittedly, it was a group with a philosophy that was clearly on the fringe of more established UFO research groups: we were attempting to initiate direct contact with aliens.

My observations of the other six members of the group told me they were highly intelligent, well mannered, sophisticated New Yorkers. Coincidentally, several of these people had backgrounds of varying importance in computers and advanced military electronics, satellites, and radar.

With us was Nicholas Voulgaris, a Field Investigator with the international UFO research group Mutual UFO Network (MUFON), who months later would become the Chief MUFON Field Investigator in New York State. I had met Nick previously at a MUFON meeting I attended along with only six people at the Commack Public Library on February 21, 2013. Nick was one of two MUFON field investigators on all of Long Island. It had long been obvious to me that UFOs did not draw much interest from the Island's seven million residents. I never understood how this could be, and I often wondered if people had been brainwashed by undetectable alien transmissions through their television sets or through some other means, maybe through our precious, pure Long Island drinking water. I could never understand how people could be so utterly disinterested in such an enormous problem as the possibility that we we're being infiltrated and studied by aliens from other planets. After all, aliens are our potential enemies. One only has to recall the Bentwaters military base case in England, in 1980, to see how easily it was for alien crafts to infiltrate a military facility that houses nuclear missiles. About eighty military personnel saw the craft at Bentwaters, right outside the Royal Air Force base at Woodbridge. This base was utilized by the 81st Fighter Wing of the United States Air Force. Not only did military personnel see spaceships and strange lights over a three-day period, sometimes inside the trees in the forest, but a staff sergeant actually touched the small craft and took notes of symbols he discovered etched into its surface.

Our CE-5 group's philosophy and method for contacting alien beings was based on the writings of Dr. Steven M. Greer, the emergency room doctor who began the Disclosure Project, a first of its kind ambitious gathering and disclosure of information from officials who have concrete knowledge about UFOs. He claims to have made successful contacts with benevolent beings from out of this world by using meditation and telepathy. He was in Phoenix, Arizona, in 1997, the day before the famous UFO episode known as the Phoenix Lights, when thousands of people encountered a UFO along a 200-mile stretch of Arizona. Some people believe Dr. Greer was the reason the spaceship visited Phoenix, showing up in a response to his invitation or mere presence in that city at that time.

As I mentioned earlier, CE-5 stands for Close Encounters of the 5th Kind. This is the kind of encounter whereby people make contact with extraterrestrials by inviting them to appear and communicate. Meditation is the key to Greer's technique. We would meditate as a group and send a beam of collective consciousness into the cosmos. Once there, through telepathy, the collective consciousness would notify aliens that we wanted to see them and communicate directly. We were relying on their ability to pick up telepathic thoughts and their advanced technology to quickly appear to us.

In my thinking, if Dr. Greer was right, then we were clearly putting ourselves at risk of actually making contact with foreign life forms, possibly jeopardizing our own lives. What if the extraterrestrials we should contact regarded humans the way humans regard spiders or rats? We were relying on their advanced minds to meet with us in peace and extend good will. Isn't this the way some people might feel as they ignore zookeepers and climb over the fence into the lions' cage to make friends with the lions—just before being pounced on and torn to shreds?

In fact, tonight the seven of us had gathered together to call alien spaceships down to Earth and for extraterrestrials to exchange information in friendship. The hope was that once the ship appeared, and the aliens were in front of us, we'd hold an intergalactic council, if you will. Through meditation, our collective consciousness would send pictures of the exact location where we were standing, with directions to the graveyard from the sky. To accomplish this, we had to picture in our minds planet Earth, then North America, then Long Island, then the area of Long Island where we were standing, then the graveyard, then our gathering of seven.

We held hands in a circle at the back of the nighttime cemetery where it was darkest and the noises of the passing cars and trucks on the nearby Long Island Expressway were the least intrusive. Chris was our leader. He was apparently the most experienced at this, having been doing it for about two years. Ron, another member of the group, had been meeting with Chris for about a year and a half to meditate on an alien visit. Though neither of them had ever made direct contact with extraterrestrials, they did claim to have paranormal experiences they chalked up to their practices with Dr. Greer's CE-5 meditation method. None of the rest of us had ever done this before, though we all had a burning interest in either UFOs or the paranormal.

Chris read a meditation from the book, *Hidden Truth: Forbidden Knowledge*, written by Dr. Greer. It was several pages long. He read it by the light of his cell phone. We had our eyes closed during this time and followed his instructions to let our minds picture ourselves leaving Earth, and even the solar system, in a second, and then returning, hopefully with aliens in tow. When Chris was finished, we let go of each other's hands and observed the sky for signs of spaceships.

At one point, Jeanne, the lone woman in the group, shone a bright searchlight into the sky to give clear direction to the spaceships that might be looking for us. Another member briefly flashed a green laser beam into the heavens, first making absolutely sure no airplanes were in the vicinity. These were not children at play with lasers; these were serious adults on a mission to make contact.

But nothing happened: no spaceships appeared, no extraterrestrials revealed themselves to us, no intergalactic council was held. We agreed to meet at a different location and try it again the following month.

10

A reporter chasing lights.

Typically, back when I was a reporter in 1989, my attire consisted of worn, brown hiking boots, tight blue jeans, a hand-crafted brown leather belt I bought in Wyoming before I married and then divorced my wife, a white shirt, and a black tie. My hair was longer, darker brown, and wild.

I often wore a gray overcoat in colder weather. It was too big, especially around the bottom, and it sort of flared out like a bell behind me. But the coat had been inexpensive to purchase on Broadway in Manhattan. It had a bizarre official look to it that I liked. The sight of the overcoat annoyed politicians, who wanted me to look neat and falsely concise like them. The overcoat had a gray belt. The belt went through loops. It had a black buckle. The politicians looked at me and chuckled when I walked into a room. I was wearing a $50 overcoat while they were wearing $800 suits. The overcoat served as a tool to let me know at a glance who my enemies—and friends—were. I didn't have many friends. It seemed I had plenty of enemies. That was fine with me. Their annoyance told me I was doing my job. You know the saying: "If you're not pissing them off, you're doing something wrong."

My preference was to leave the coat open with the belt unbuckled. The back of the coat whooshed in the wind. It trailed behind me as I shot up marble stairs into loud crowded meeting rooms and flew through the halls of government, where politicians didn't look happy to see me. In the overcoat's big right pocket was a small black tape recorder; in the other, a pen and a long reporter's notepad, blue and white.

A laminated Suffolk County Police Department press badge hung around my neck. The image in the center of the pass was a shield that looked like a cop's badge. The shield was purposely big and imposing, so it was easy for cops to spot at a crime scene, where a lot of people might be gathered and a lot of excitement might be confusing everything. They'd let me through the lines. Intimidating bold black letters written across the badge announced, PRESS.

Most days found me sleeping late and beginning my workdays after lunchtime. But that's only because I worked straight through the night till my head grew weary for sleep and I had to lie down. By then, a pale dawn was usually breaking in the eastern sky. Coffee kept me going. People think reporters spend most of their time writing at their desks. But writing is only a small part of a reporter's job. The bulk of our work is in the field, out talking to people, looking at things, sizing up problems. It's all done on behalf of the people, but some of us are also compulsive writers, writing about things we see on the streets. I probably fit into that latter group.

In my car was a police scanner. Another handheld police scanner was usually lost somewhere amid a pile of newspapers and maps on my cluttered desk at home. If something interesting was happening that I heard over the scanner, I'd dig the radio out of the clutter and carry it around the house with me—when I took a shower, for example, or when I was out of my car and sitting in the fresh night air of the Pine Barrens, looking up at the white glinting stars in the black, velvet sky. The scanners broadcast information about current police matters in Suffolk County. Officers talked over their radios about emergencies happening at that minute, like missing people, kidnappings, robberies, burglaries, bar fights, murders, traffic problems, domestic disputes—you name it.

Sometimes the cops even talked about unexplainable lights seen in the sky.

Naturally, for a cop, every night has troubles of its own. I listened to my car scanner as I drove alone through the blackened woods of the pine forest with the narrow canyon of lighter night sky overhead, lighting my way between the trees. A blanket of stars, bathed in the glorious background haze of the silver-dust Milky Way, drew me hypnotically deeper into the twisted trees. I often pursued the strange lights the cops discussed across the airways. You could tell the officers were embarrassed to associate themselves with the reports because people with scanners, like me, could hear them talking about them. I thought maybe writing stories about the unexplainable lights seen over the Pine Barrens would make for interesting reading, so I went out alone at night looking for them.

My eyes scanned the night sky through my car's windshield as I drove slowly around the winding bends of midnight to see what the complainants were talking about when they described to police dispatchers the strange, glowing lights in the sky over the trees. Mostly these instances were reported by people who lived in old log cabins and rustic bungalows isolated deep inside the woods in the dark forest. Some people used to refer to these folks as Long Island hillbillies because they had outhouses and well-water pumps. It was said they were descendants of people who drifted to these woods from outcroppings of Squiretown, a very old area of Red Creek near Flanders, many generations back. There are very few, if any, of these hillbillies left these days.

Sometimes I spotted bright stars moving over the trees or sometimes inside them. Of course, now I know they were not moving stars, but spaceships like the one seen by eighty military personal during the three-day period in the Rendlesham Forest in Suffolk, England in late December 1980, as mentioned earlier.

11

Chasing a mountain lion in the Pine Barrens.

This is how I learned first-hand about UFOs visiting the Pine Barrens: One summer when I was a reporter I chased stories of a mountain lion. Some of the hillbillies who lived in log cabins claimed to have seen a mountain lion running loose in the sandy woods of the Pine Barrens. Long Island hasn't seen the likes of mountain lions living naturally on its land in probably something like a thousand years, if ever. We used to have black bear in our woods, and many species of whales in our waters, but they're all gone now.

Here's an essential Long Island geography lesson: at one time, the Pine Barrens covered about a quarter million acres of Long Island, just like they do in southern New Jersey today. Mankind's encroachment into the woods reduced Long Island's Pine Barrens to just over 100,000 acres by the year 2000. The precious woods were headed for ruin. But when you least expected it, they were preserved by the state's passing of the Pine Barrens Preservation Act. It was a last minute reprieve by Governor Mario Cuomo.

The Pine Barrens are areas of pitch pine and scrub oak trees critical to the good health of Long Island's drinking water. Long Island is very sandy. The roots of these special trees bind the sandy ground in such a way that rainwater is filtered cleanly through the sand on its way down to underground aquifers. The spots where rainwater filters down to the aquifers are known as "recharge areas." The process of recharging the aquifers actually takes hundreds of years. That's how long it takes a drop of water to reach the aquifers. It all starts the second raindrops hit the ground in the Pine Barrens.

Long Island's three aquifers hold trillions of gallons of some of the purest water in the United States. According to the state, almost all Long Island gets its water from these aquifers. Nobody, or very few people on Long Island, drink water from reservoirs like people do in nearby Manhattan. The aquifers are composed of water from melted ice that was trapped under enormous waves of rock and dirt during the ice age that ended 11,000 years ago. The debris the Wisconsin Glaciation pushed across the continent and dropped here is now Long Island. That's how this island arrived. That's how the ice underneath Long Island was trapped. That's how we got trillions of gallons of pure water. Some people have suggested the aliens that visit out-island want our water. But I think they want much more than that.

Locals I interviewed, who claimed to have seen the mountain lion in the Pine Barrens forest, said the big cat must have been raised in someone's garage and was probably set free because it became too unruly and troublesome for its owner to deal with any longer. There was already a precedent for a mountain lion raised in a home on Long Island: years earlier, a man allegedly illegally housed a mountain lion in his home till the police were called to get it out. The big cat was immediately sent off to the zoo at the Brookhaven Town Holtsville Ecology Site, where it lived for many years, pacing back and forth non-stop in its green-barred cage, trying to figure a way out.

One white-haired old lady living alone in a log bungalow in the woods of the expansive Pine Barrens of Manorville—in the densely treed Central Pine Barrens Region—said she saw the puma in the glow of her yellow back porch light. She claimed the lethal cat was crouching sneakily down as it ran with its big paws through her backyard at night—there was a wild, black turkey in its mouth.

I traveled the winding back roads of the mysterious forest most nights till near dawn for weeks chasing after the mountain lion. But I never saw it. The cat seemed to just vanish after the last report came in about it having the dead turkey in its mouth.

Halsey Manor Road in the lonely Pine Barrens of Manorville. This is a typical lonely road in the pine woods of eastern Long Island. It's on just such a road that lights of UFOs are often seen at night.

An investigator with the New York State Department of Environmental Conservation (DEC), whom I interviewed for a story about the mountain lion, told me that I would never see the animal "because it's just too damn smart." He said the Pine Barrens forest was a good place for a big cat, such as a mountain lion, to hide. The sheer vastness of the land would protect it, he said. The peripheral land around the forest was sparsely populated and also heavily treed, adding further protection, he told me.

Years later, I would interview experts about the Jersey Devil in the Pine Barrens of New Jersey and they would tell me the same thing about that notorious beast. One-third of New Jersey is Pine Barrens, or "Pinelands," as locals call them. Nonetheless, over 2,000 people have reported either seeing or in some way experiencing the Jersey Devil since 1735. It flew over towns and, in 1909, firemen even shot water from a fire hose at it when it swooped down at them.

Is the Jersey Devil possibly like the Long Island Devil—an extraterrestrial that got stuck here on Earth because of a spaceship crash? I want to find the Long Island Devil and try to communicate with it. I want to find out where it's from. Clearly, the Long Island Devil, if it exists, is a smart creature, much smarter than even a mountain lion.

I never did see the mountain lion, but I got to know the Pine Barrens intimately. I learned the contours of its lonely roads twisting through the seemingly endless trees. If I passed even one car in an hour those nights I would have been surprised.

It was creepy being all alone in the deep of the night, miles away from a town or village or even a house. Never were there any street lights on the foreboding roads, and nobody was ever behind me or in front of me on the tar; nobody anywhere—just me and the breeze-blown, haunted trees.

Sometimes I'd just pull off the road and park the car in a patch of sand under a pine tree and hike into the woods with a flashlight. Who cares? Who's going to stop me? I'd find a spot a mile into the trees to sit and watch the full moon, listen to the breezes, the owls hooting, the occasional hoofs of whitetail deer hitting the sandy ground somewhere nearby, the cicadas, crickets, and the strange sudden silences. My breath would fly up in cold mists like ghosts into the frigid air of pre-dawn.

One early dawn, I came out of the woods to find the back window of my car blown out. Money, sitting in an open compartment below the dashboard, was not touched. The police officer who I showed the windows to when I drove to the Sixth Precinct, at that time located in Coram, noted that the window was blown *out* of the car, not smashed *in*. The violence to the window occurred within the car, not from outside.

"God-damned strangest thing I'd ever seen," said the officer.

He didn't file a complaint because he said that since the doors were locked and humans didn't do it, there was no need to complain to anyone about it. He didn't blame me. I think he had seen this sort of thing before in the Pine Barrens, though he said he hadn't.

I discovered a secret, too. Sometimes lights from silent crafts shone over the trees in the Pine Barrens. These crafts were neither airplanes nor helicopters. I don't believe they were of human origin.

12

Lights of crafts over the Pine Barrens.

The realization that we humans were being visited by beings that were not human, and probably from some other planet, from a civilization obviously more advanced than our own, made me shudder. They had spaceships that made it all the way to Earth. How did they do that?

The crafts I saw those nights over the trees were not thunderous like the fireball I witnessed on the day of the Great New York Blackout of 1965. The ships were silent, and without obvious propulsion systems. They had no wings or tails. I froze when I saw the blue, yellow, orange, and red lights.

I'd creep out of the woods, hiding behind trees so I could see the vehicles. Each had different colored lights: often blue, sometimes just white, sometimes all colors. I never did see exactly how all the crafts were shaped. Sometimes I could tell they were only yards in diameter and circular, but I couldn't tell how tall they were or if they were classic disk-shaped or were parts of larger ships that I could not see in the dark. Other times I could tell they were large, and I sensed they were not circular. In all these cases, I only saw the lights and occasional glints off their black surfaces.

I'm pretty sure the space beings in these ships saw me, though. That is, I felt like they saw me because I believe they let me know telepathically that it was all right that I saw their ships, but that I should not say anything. The feeling that I was being observed was not from me, not psychological, that is. Rather, it was from them watching me. Now, I know this to be true. It's called telepathy— beings communicating directly to a person inside his or her head.

One of the things they let me know as I hid from them in the woods was that my emotions change the colors of the lights on their crafts. The very skins of the crafts change colors in response to my feelings at any particular minute. I don't know how I can explain I knew this, other than to say it was telepathy. I don't know why the aliens would even care how I felt emotionally, no less change the colors of their spaceships in my honor, but from what they told me through their magic communication skills, they did. These voices I was hearing were not unlike my own thoughts in my own familiar mental voice, but the thoughts were not mine. They were thoughts communicated to me from an outside source. The apparatus of my brain channeled these thoughts into my consciousness. At the same time, my very being alerted me to the invasion of my mind by an ungodly and unknown entity or entities. It's a chilling, stomach-churning experience because it's a no-nonsense invasion of one's own certitudes, while also being extremely interesting and even comforting because it leaves the door open for hope that there is more out there in the universe than what we know. This might explain my reluctant excitement receiving the uninvited messages. One thing's for sure: they know me.

13

Not easy to explain.

I kept all this to myself. Even about the broken car window. I told nobody. I had no proof the lights skimming the tops of the pine tress were spaceships or that the force of low vibrations from the crafts or from something else I could not detect blew the window out of my car. For all I knew, the lights could have been natural atmospheric events that occur regularly over the Pine Barrens because of electromagnetic energies caused by all the water underneath the trees—or something else—that I didn't understand because I am not a scientist. I could easily explain away the telepathy by telling myself that my imagination was getting the better part of me because I was in a known paranormally charged environment. After all, the Pine Barrens are known to be the walking grounds of ghosts. For many decades, people claimed the Pine Barrens forest was haunted by a variety of ghosts and ghouls. There are many Indian burial grounds in the woods. Diane Hill and I have seen a ghoul there, as described in our book *Ghosts, Ghouls, and Monsters of Long Island*, but that's another story. We have seen ghosts here, too; we've written about them in the three books we've published since 2009.

14

Politics in the Pine Barrens.

Meanwhile, during this time, builders scowled at me in the aisles of the Planning Department offices at town halls. They were the biggest and busiest offices in the local town governments because this was where all the action in the towns was taking place. Developers were falling all over themselves to construct huge housing developments in the remaining pristine pine woods. So much of Brookhaven, Riverhead, and Southampton Townships are Pine Barrens that the townships were deluged with site plans from builders seeking hurried approvals from different boards in the respective towns, like the planning boards, zoning boards, and town boards.

When they saw me, the builders turned to each other and mumbled, then looked back at me with scorn in their eyes. They knew I was there to rake over their building site plans for the monster housing developments they proposed for the fragile Pine Barrens.

In the county legislature building in Hauppauge, slick-haired politicians played with change in their expensive suit pants pockets while they tried to stare me down and curse me under their breath to their crones. I *whooshed* through the hallways. I was there to uncover the dirt. I did the best I could with what I had. I wondered if they knew the Pine Barrens were the home of spaceships.

PART II

CHAPTER FOUR

2013

Alien Telepathic Trickery?

15

A UFO appears.

My ghost hunting partner, Diane Hill, is of recent years also my reluctant UFO investigations partner. At this point, as I've mentioned, we have been writing books and articles about the paranormal and speaking together for a decade.

The event I'm about to relate was the incident I think of as signaling my awareness of aliens in spaceships communicating with me, as they probably have been doing my whole life without me realizing it. Therefore, it is also the event that led me to the belief aliens have invaded Long Island.

It was late. I was driving to Diane's house in my black SUV. Only an hour had passed since the failed attempt to contact extraterrestrials in Almshouse Cemetery (Potter's Field Cemetery) in Yaphank with my fellow CE-5 partners. I was going to stay at Diane's house overnight. I often do.

Diane lives in bustling West Hempstead, not far from the border of Queens, which is the beginning of New York City to the west. No doubt she was going to have a lot of questions about my experience that night in the graveyard with the CE-5 group. It was the first time I had ever done CE-5 mediation and, once it was over, even *I* had thought it was preposterous to think we were going to make contact with space people. So, I thought, *Just wait till Diane rips into me with jokes and snide remarks about making contact with ET.* I was prepared

11th Street in Garden City. It was across the street from the large parking lot (above) to the left side of the building (below) that Joseph Flammer saw a jumbo jet hang motionless in the sky—or was it a spaceship creating the illusion of an airplane?

for her sarcastic smirks and ridicule. I guess I deserved as much. It was sophomoric of me to think extraterrestrials would answer our calls for them to appear.

After leaving the cold, dark graveyard, I drove about forty minutes on the Long Island Expressway west to Exit 39, Glen Cove Road, and drove to Old Country Road, then made a right towards the court house in Mineola, and then a left on Washington Avenue, then another right. This put me less than ten minutes away from Diane's house.

As I was driving on 11th Street in Garden City on my way to nearby West Hempstead, I noticed extraordinarily bright, flashing lights of a mega airplane in the sky. The super jumbo jet was close and enormous, like a traveling city unto itself. The plane was moving very slowly and I thought it was also too low over the area. I grew worried. Was it going to crash? Was it going to crash into *me*?

What was most striking about the suddenly appearing craft was that its pulsating lights were all white, and brighter and larger than I had ever noticed on any other airplane I had ever seen.

Airplanes in the sky in this area of Long Island are common because JFK International Airport is just a short distance to the southwest. At any given moment in this area of Nassau County, one can look up to the heavens and spot at least five or six airplanes circling to land at JFK, or climbing up and away from the busy airport, or descending to make a landing.

At first I slowed my SUV down, since in my rear-view mirror I saw no one else was on the dark road behind me, and there was no one in front of me. So I observed the bright lights in the sky, trying to understand why they were so bright and large and all white. After all, didn't planes have different colored lights: red and green, or red and blue? I was puzzled.

Finally, I pulled over to the side of the road and opened the vehicle's window so I had a clear view. The thing is, I immediately noticed there was no noise coming from the craft. Then I realized the giant airplane was not moving at all. It was just hanging in the sky, like it was a cut-out from a children's coloring book and then pasted in space: an enormous jumbo jet with bright, white, flashing lights making no noise at all—just hanging motionlessly in the sky!

I stared at the craft in disbelief for many seconds until it dawned on me with complete comprehension in a sudden flash that I was being shown a secret. It was an epiphany that seemed to come from some source other than my own brain. The amazing secret I was being shown was that aliens disguise their space crafts to look just like jets in the sky. This allows them to go undetected by Earthlings. It's not that the alien crafts are actually reshaped to look just like airplanes. Rather, it's that the aliens set up smoke screens, probably in our minds through some form of telepathic hypnosis, creating fake pictures in the sky, and behind the smoke screens, the illusions, are the real crafts. They make us see airplanes when in fact they're not airplanes at all!

"How could they do this?" I uttered.

If extraterrestrials really do communicate telepathically, then this was the first true direct telepathic message I ever received about the nature of aliens. The messages I received when I was a reporter watching spaceships over the Pine Barrens in the late 1980s and early 1990s were far less consequential. Here I was being given real information about our space visitors.

Nearly two months later, on April 18, 2013, I'd call upon a long-haired teenage girl in my audience at Hicksville Public Library, where I was delivering a solo lecture about UFOs visiting Long Island, and she told me she was in her mother's car and looked up at a jet that seemed too close, too big, and with too many pulsating, white lights to be a real jet, and she watched it just hang in the sky motionless and without any sound for a long while, and knew somehow, magically, this was a disguise for alien spaceships amongst us. I had not shared my own experience with her nor anybody else in the audience, so I knew she was not patronizing me. When I heard her words, my training in the paranormal told me that what she was saying was a message intended for me as validation of my experience with the motionless jet I saw over Garden City. She may not have even been aware that she was saying the words, for they might have been inspired by the aliens and merely said through her. If you think this is impossible or highly improbable, think again.

At first, I thought the aliens were possibly mocking me through the teenage girl, repeating my own experience exactly. Then I realized I was being shown bits of information that would one day serve as a primer for understanding alien wisdom and knowledge and thus allowing me to grow in my own wisdom and knowledge. At least, that's what I wanted to believe. The reality was that I was being fed information according to how and when the aliens saw fit, for their benefit, not mine, no doubt. The girl was a prop to let me know I am, in fact, being contacted and that the aliens were watching my reactions to their contact.

At any rate, I was stunned as I watched the motionless airplane over Garden City. The size of the craft was larger than any airplane I had ever seen up close. The event was interrupted when I noticed the headlights of a police car flash in the large empty municipal parking lot across from Sears on 11th Street. The officer in the car should have seen the big jet in the sky over the lot, but I knew intuitively that he had not. My feeling was that the police officer was about to drive over to me to ask what I was doing because I had come to a dead stop in the middle of a perfectly good lane at night with my head sticking out the driver's side window. Maybe the cop thought I needed help and he was about to come over. Strangely, I didn't want him to know about the secret I'd just discovered. This seemed to be part of the telepathic message: *Don't tell anyone.* I have since come to believe that telling people about what happens to you when you are a Contactee is the first step to resisting.

So I drove to the corner of 11th Street and Franklin Avenue and crossed over Franklin Avenue under the traffic light and, with squealing tires, quickly pulled into an empty parking lot behind a group of stores. In a hurry, I turned the vehicle around so I faced the street at the sidewalk. From the edge of the parking lot I searched the sky for the motionless mega jumbo jet I had seen only fifteen seconds earlier and had been watching for at least two minutes. But it was no longer there. It was nowhere in the sky now. I watched the sky for minutes. I got out of the SUV and walked on the sidewalk, looking for the plane. But the craft had vanished. Where it went was a mystery, because it had been hanging like the moon in the empty night sky, brilliant and silent. How and why it appeared to me was a complete mystery.

A little over a month later, I would be reviewing MUFON Case #46472 (found on www.Mufon.com and also listed with the UFO Sightings Report Center, www. UFOsightingsreport.com, as Case 116750, https://www.sightingsreport.com/sightings/116750), in which I found an interesting parallel to my own experience with the telepathic message I received in Garden City. The report was from a man who said he was driving with his wife in the countryside of Oregon in 2009 when he looked up and saw a UFO stationary in the sky over a field wherein cows grazed. He said the UFO looked like two disks put together with louvers on top. He sent MUFON a CAD-created image of the craft he saw.

As he looked up at the UFO over the farmlands of Oregon, the man said he received a telepathic message not to look up at the spaceship or acknowledge what he saw as a UFO, but to look away to the cows, the grass, and the overall environment, then to go home, and forget he ever saw the UFO. Four years later, after remembering the details of the sighting and compiling a representation of the UFO with a 3D CAD program at work, he filed his report with MUFON with an accompanying computer generated picture. He claimed the space vehicle "cloaked" as he watched it.

Here is the man's actual story:

> We were heading North on I-5, and exited on the Brooks Exit #293. Pulled to the stop sign and normally I just roll through while looking left. This time, I just stopped and stared at the (rough looking) double-stacked plate disk with louvers on top and no landing gear. I told myself to get a good description of it; then, by the time I had stared at it for less than a minute, it cloaked. It looked just like a blink of an eye—only my eye did not blink. As it was cloaking I received a telepathic message that I saw nothing unusual, see the cows, and the irrigation equipment, and the buildings in the background, the green grass; my attention was purposely redirected to other things instead of what I just saw.

In my reading of the UFO report over the Oregon farmlands, I found the following comment posted by a reader from England on the subject of the telepathic message the witness received:

> I found this report very interesting because of the (subliminal?) telepathic message, telling the witness he was seeing nothing— to look at other things. I recall someone going into an old quarry, where they had seen a UFO descend into (source: book by Timothy Good?). The witness found nothing, but briefly noticed an old portacabin, partly hidden in shadows, to one side as he passed it by. He gave up his search and left the quarry. However, later he realized that he was somehow, being "told" that the structure in the shadows "was a portacabin"

and hence ignore it….Just thought this correlation of telepathic trickery might help. (Comment from Fred CC from York, N. Yorkshire, UK).

Then, as I researched deeper, I found out that on the night I was in the graveyard with the CE-5 group, two UFOs were spotted over West Hempstead, the very hamlet in which Diane lives, and also the very place neighboring Garden City, where I saw the hanging jumbo jet that same night. This was also the place I was sleeping that night. A UFO report was filed with MUFON (Case #45983). Not only were the oddities spotted directly over the exact area where Diane lives, but a video posted on UFO Sightings Report Center proves the strange red balls of light in the sky were recorded from a parking lot across the street from where Diane lives!

This is the report from March 1, 2013 of UFOs over West Hempstead:

While standing in a shopping center parking lot, myself and wife noticed a large fireball; initial impression was it was a hot-air balloon–size sphere combusting. But the fireball never burned out; there was no smoke, contrail, or sound. We then noticed a second fireball seemingly traveling adjacent to the first offset diagonally. Both objects traveled at approximately 80 to 110 mph, seemingly slower than a typical helicopter in flight. The objects traveled in unison, maintaining a constant distance from each other in a straight, possibly slightly ascending flight, but below a night overcast sky. The objects were observed below a dense cloud cover. Airplanes were observed in the sky at the same time as the objects, but not in close proximity.

Did the UFOs visit West Hempstead on the night of the CE-5 meeting because I was going there, and was this happening because I and other members of the CE-5 group that met in the graveyard asked aliens to appear to us? And had aliens telepathically communicated with me to let me know they are here on Earth, but to keep quiet about it? Why would they do that?

Strange things were only beginning to happen. The following months would be filled with bizarre, unexplainable occurrences that I can only reason away as the result of asking aliens to communicate with me. What followed in the days immediately to come would also make me suspect I was being visited by Men in Black—that is, extraterrestrials watching me.

CHAPTER FIVE

ANTI-UFO ARMY HELICOPTERS VISIT ROCKY POINT

16

Helicopter chasing UFO over my neighborhood.

So, on Monday night (March 3, 2013), only forty-eight hours since I'd seen the motionless airplane hanging like the moon in the sky over Garden City and had received the telepathic message I related prior, I was in my home in Rocky Point. I was roused out of comfort from my couch by the alarming, gargantuan thunder of a large helicopter's thudding blades. It was over my house!

I paused the DVD player. I had been watching a documentary about Jack Kerouac that I had taken out of the library that day. The room was dark except for the bright image of poor soulful mad Jack's literary face paused on the television set. The thunderous helicopter was a great contradiction to his poetic sadness and playfulness. I had the wooden blinds covering the big window at the front of the house set down and the slits open so they would let the sunlight into the room in the morning, the way I like.

I ran to the door at the left side of the living room, which is the main door I use to come and go from the house. It opens up to a large brick porch. I opened the door and stood outside on the big stone porch to see what the matter could be. The helicopter, which I felt was probably military because of its monster-like size, sat in the forlorn sky over my house. It suddenly swung its bright beam hungrily down upon me. I shielded my eyes and lunged back inside the living room, afraid that I was going to be mistaken for the bloodthirsty thief the authorities were probably searching for; and, of course, they would end up shooting me instead of that man who they were really hunting. The helicopter then moved off, and I stepped back outside and watched it rip over the neighborhood with the silver-tipped clouds in the moonlit sky behind it.

The thunderous craft slowly circled the area of my neighborhood twice with its searchlights burning up houses, cars, and trees before it returned to my house and hovered in the sky at an angle to it with the searchlight flaring upon my roof and invading my windows, right into the rooms of my home like poisonous gas. Blinding white light, slotted by the blinds, scorched through my living room windows and bleached out the floors and walls. I darted back inside the house and flew into a room where the snaking bright light could not illuminate me, closing the door and hiding behind the wall, hoping not to be killed. I was now a target in my own house. I removed the cell phone in my pocket. I'd call the police to ask them what they wanted. But the helicopter moved slowly off again. I looked at the cell phone's clock. It was 10:29.

At 10:35, the helicopter returned for a third and final time, blaring its powerful atomic searchlight into my house. The entire property was flooded in its light. The chopper's cutting blades thudded like angry giants thrusting swords overhead. When the helicopter finally flew off again, I saw that the spotlight was now searching the sky above it, and I thought I saw something there, maybe a disk-shaped thing, but I couldn't really make it out because it looked dark. Nonetheless, the helicopter seemed to rush urgently off in pursuit of the object. That was the last I saw of the helicopter that night.

I had lived for thirty-five years in the same house and never once had a helicopter aim a spotlight into my living room windows. In fact, I don't recall a helicopter ever searching my neighborhood for anything. It was definitely a first. What troubled me most about the experience was that it seemed my house was the epicenter of the search, and this took place only two days after I had stood with the six others in a dark graveyard and called upon space aliens to pay us a visit. In my case, they did visit me in Garden City. I'm certain of that now. But were aliens also in the disk above the helicopter? Where they in my neighborhood because they were there for me?

Were the soldiers in the helicopter federal agents? Were they from a secretive branch of the military, like the ones who reportedly were present at Southaven Park when a spaceship supposedly crashed there? Could they be soldiers from an army that exists outside of the regular U.S. Army? I had read about these fellows. Maybe they were headquartered in a secret place like Area 51 and were trained to carry out secret missions to fight the aliens. Who were they? What were they looking for? Why were strange inexplicable things, like the jet, hanging above Garden City, and the UFOs spotted over West Hempstead the same night, and now this helicopter over my house suddenly happening to me? Later, I would call the public information desk of the Suffolk County Police Department, only to be told there was no information available about the helicopters in my neighborhood on that date.

Especially interesting to me was the fact that MUFON had received a report of an incident that happened on Long Island involving a helicopter chasing a UFO that took place only three weeks after my experience. Strikingly similar to my experience, a person claimed to see a helicopter chasing a bright orb in the sky over King's Park (also on the North Shore of Long Island, but probably thirty miles west of where I live in Rocky Point).

According to the witness who filed MUFON Case #46449:

> Was at friends house, went outside to hear a helicopter that sounded like a military one. I've seen them come over my town before. So me and my friend wait to see this just above the trees. My friend goes "WTF look!" I see this thing that looks like a star in front of the helicopter, like about no more than 100 feet away. It had a really thin trail coming from it…

17

The big questions.

Could it possibly be that because I stood in a graveyard at night and called upon extraterrestrials to reveal themselves that they were now actually communicating with me in the form of telepathic messages and showing me they were keeping tabs on me? Were they drawing government agents to me? Were the agents in the helicopter from some kind of Anti-UFO Army? Was the information I received in the telepathic message about airplanes serving as mirages to trick humans delivered to me by those beings that received our call in the cosmos on that night of the CE-5 meeting?

I lay awake in bed till four in the morning in the hours after the aforementioned helicopter bathed my house in light three separate times, observing every flash of light from the occasional car headlights that moved down my street, from the bouncing shadows of the tall tree limbs in the yellow street light outside my house that danced into my windows and on my walls like Halloween ghosts. I listened to the whispers in the wind and the creaking of the old wood house settling, wondering if I would suddenly turn this way or that and spot the shape of a Gray standing beside the bed in the dark, suddenly sensing its telepathic message for me not to resist. I envisioned being carried out against my will into a silver spaceship in a fog, where I'd be examined by a stainless steel anal probe, and then left naked on my front lawn, only to wake up in the morning with neighbors gaping at me and laughing. This is exactly what Stan Romanek claimed happened to him often, less than a decade ago. He wrote a book called *Messages: The Worlds Most Documented Extraterrestrial Contact Story,* in which he tells readers he was given mathematical formulas to give to scientists, which he did. In the pages of the book he exhibits photographs he took of the aliens looking into his home's windows.

Where would all this go for me? Is it really possible to make contact with an alien race from another planet, possibly from anther galaxy, simply by calling them down? And was our government, with its classified secrets about UFOs, actually protecting us with its secrecy? Has our government been in communication with aliens but judged them to be potentially toxic poison to us? Was our government on the job for our benefit, seeking a solution, trying to shield us from worry and fear of the truth as best it could? I have always assumed the government was keeping what it knew about UFOs secret because the information would only prove harmful to us if made public. Of course, it's always been a challenge to try to figure out what the government knows about extraterrestrials that we don't. And it's always been a mystery why the government so emphatically denies the existence of UFOs. Some people might suggest the government is in communication with aliens and actually receives a military edge from studying their technology, and thus it wants to keep that edge secret. I do hope this is not the case. In this instance, though it might sound ludicrous, I think we have to put our trust in our government—that they know what they are doing and are working to protect us, though we may not agree with their methods of disinformation and denial. Remember, government agents have families, too.

18

Strange figure appears and disappears.

The third day after the CE-5 meeting in the graveyard was a rainy, miserable, gray day. I was thankful I was off work, so I could take care of some chores around the house.

I walked around the rooms on the first floor, unshowered, in old, blue sweats and a brown robe. I figured: damn all, the government ruined my movie about Kerouac last night. At least I'm going to be comfortable on this bleak, cold day. At one point, at dusk, I looked out my door window and saw a large nondescript figure standing off to the side of my property, looking towards my house. It looked like the figure was wearing a brown cape the size of a blanket. People often walked down the street, so initially, I wasn't concerned. But as I watched the figure move off and disappear on the road behind the bulk of an old trailer in my yard, I grew more concerned. In other words, I noticed the figure did not emerge from the other side of said trailer. It did not go into the trailer because the place where it was walking was at least fifty feet behind it.

Where had the brown figure gone? And was it a man I saw or was it something else? I immediately ran outside, and without taking my eyes off the road ahead of me, I ran behind the trailer and studied the empty road. In my thinking, the figure had simply disappeared.

I admit I was starting to get a little jumpy. Strange things were happening that I couldn't explain. And it seemed to be happening ever since I called aliens to Earth with the other members of the CE-5 group in the graveyard.

19

Group breaks into paranormal babble.

The following Saturday, I worked my regular evening shift at the group home for developmentally disabled adults in Ridge, where I had been employed as an instructor for ten years. At one point, all six employees on shift that night gathered in the kitchen to prepare snacks for the ten residents of the home. A new employee, a young lady with strange, faraway, alien-looking eyes, singled me out of the group and began telling me—for no obvious reason—that she had many paranormal experiences, including seeing UFOs and Grays. She had no knowledge that I was involved in researching such phenomena. She had no knowledge that I had written books and articles about the paranormal.

It should be mentioned that nobody particularly trusted this new employee because she was odd and fell asleep a few times while sitting in the home's living room. She was headed down a bad path as an employee, and we didn't think she would last long.

As the young lady launched into telling me about her experiences, she moved ever closer to me and looked ever deeper into my eyes, as if she wanted to extract something from inside me, making me feel deeply uncomfortable. I am a person who enjoys private space around me. "I saw things," she began. Her eyes were black, without other colors, I thought as I looked at her.

At that exact moment a ruckus arose in the center of the kitchen. I turned to see the other five employees in the room had formed a circle, each talking over the others, all sharing their own paranormal experiences. It was as if they were speaking in tongues. They seemed to each pick out a person to speak to inside the circle, then just let go, unconcerned that they were talking over their fellow employees. I'm certain no one among them heard any details of the others' stories because none of them was listening to anybody else. I couldn't' make any sense of all the gibberish.

Naturally, I assumed this was another event inspired by extraterrestrials for my education. For some reason, lessons unraveled before my eyes regularly now, but for what ultimate purpose? I couldn't say.

While the young lady with the extraterrestrial black eyes continued telling me her bizarre experiences, up close to my body, the group of employees in the circle in the kitchen continued their babbling, unaffected by the obvious fact that nobody was listening to anybody else because they were all talking at the same time. By now, I was completely ignoring the girl beside me and focused on the random pandemonium that had erupted in the room. The employees at the center of the kitchen were like five tape recorders going off simultaneously. I watched in utter amazement. They had no awareness of what they were doing. It might have been funny, if it wasn't so frightening.

After several minutes of this most abnormal behavior, the circle broke in an instant, and each of the employees went about their business of quietly preparing food for the residents. They didn't seem to have any conscious awareness of what they had just done. The girl at my side simply walked away as if a wire had been pulled, and all was quiet, back to normal. I had never witnessed such an event in all my life. I came in the next day to learn that the strange girl who started all the odd behavior had been fired because her general strangeness was believed to be drug related. But I'd wager her strangeness was alien inspired.

20

Man in black.

I spent the last week of March with Diane at her house in West Hempstead, so she wouldn't be alone at night. The neighborhood had gone down in recent years and crime was on the upswing.

On the second afternoon while staying at Diane's house, I heard banging at the front door, as if someone was trying to get in. Diane was at work.

I went downstairs and opened the front door just in time to see a black car pull away. A man with a gray shirt was driving. I couldn't see his face.

The next day, Diane and I decided to get out and take care of some errands. Upon stepping out of the house, we noticed a thin, balding man with glasses awkwardly taking pictures of the house next to Diane's with a small silver camera. Diane didn't know this man. She had never seen him before. The man paused to glance at us, then went down to the next house in the line and took a photograph of it, too. Then he went down to the next house. We had probably missed him by only seconds taking a photograph of Diane's house as he went down the row of houses on her block.

"Why is he taking pictures of all the houses on my street?" Diane asked. "He doesn't have permission to do that!"

"I don't know why," I said, "but I'll ask him."

"No," Diane insisted, "don't!"

We watched the man move towards the house on the corner near a busy Westminster Road. This was the area where the couple had video recorded two fireballs crossing West Hempstead on the night I saw the airplane hanging motionless in the sky over Garden City, just a week or so before.

Diane started her car and drove up the block towards the man. His worn face showed a lot of teeth, as if his mouth was permanently opened in a sneer. He wore a green jacket and a gray shirt.

As we approached, the man turned the corner behind some bushes and walked a short distance, then stopped and watched traffic pass on Westminster Road. When he saw us observing him, he started to run the other way on the sidewalk, then stopped short, looked across the road, looked at us, then grabbed an opening in traffic and skipped across the road towards National Wholesale Liquidators, the big store located on the corner of Hempstead Turnpike and Westminster Road.

Now he *definitely* had our interest. We followed him into the huge busy parking lot of National Wholesale Liquidators and pulled into a spot right next to the store, just as the toothy, balding, thin man entered the building. He stopped in front of a large window facing us. We believed he had been only pretending to study cases of Snapple on sale that were piled before the window. No doubt he was observing us. Then he disappeared into the store.

We waited twenty minutes for the man to re-emerge from the building, but he did not reappear. I wanted to go in and see what he was up to, but Diane pleaded with me not to do that.

We reasoned that if the man was legitimately shopping, he wouldn't be able to buy many products because it didn't seem to us that he had a way to transport the items home, since he was on foot and apparently did not have a car nearby.

We left, hoping to never see the man again.

21

Lake erupts with unexplainable ripples.

The next afternoon was warm and sunny. Spring was finally edging its way out of cold winter. Diane and I decided to get out and take a walk at Hempstead Lake State Park. We often walk there to stretch our legs and clear our heads. We'd walk up towards the reservoir, past the dog lawn, around the large pond, and then through the woods back to our car.

But this afternoon, when we passed the reservoir, we saw something that neither of us had ever seen before. The water in the reservoir was behaving in a manner that seemed entirely unnatural. It was rippling extremely quickly, in circles in all directions from a few different spots, as if things unseen were hovering just above the water, pulsating over it; and their rapidly pulsating propulsion systems pounded the water in short, quick bursts from above. Or maybe it was one large object that had several propulsion units located in different areas of its structure and these were hitting the water with vibrations. Ripples shot far and wide in an unnaturally fast manner and in a way we had never seen water ripple before—the energy hitting the water came from above, not below.

As we stood under the trees on the reservoir's bank and watched this unfamiliar phenomenon, we discussed the possibilities of underground streams having an effect on the water. No, we agreed, that wasn't the cause. We discussed other possible causes, including fish, turtles, frogs, or bugs causing the ripples. When we expressed doubt to each other about these possible causes, we hypothesized that gas bubbles from under the water were causing havoc at the surface. In the end, we didn't accept any of the possible explanations we came up with as plausible.

Eventually, one by one, these oddities in the water ended and the surface fell calm and serene again, leaving us confused as to what we had just seen, or thought we had seen. We shook our heads, shrugged our shoulders, and went on with our walk.

22

Men in Black crash into each other on street.

On the way home, we were stopped at a red light on a side street that approached busy Wakefield Avenue, located in the heart of the small hamlet of Lakeview. This side street was empty of traffic and the sidewalks were absent of people. The red light seemed oddly long for such a lonely place.

As we sat there waiting for the light to change to green so we could go about our lives, I suddenly observed a man with a shaved head exiting a wide walkway from a blue building on the corner on the right side of the street in front of us.

As he turned right onto the sidewalk from the building's walkway, another man unexpectedly appeared from out of nowhere and brushed up against him. The second man who brushed up against the first man did this as he turned left from the sidewalk and up the walkway towards the building. I didn't notice the second man on the street before he appeared and brushed up against the first guy. At that second, I had been observing the very area where he appeared, and he hadn't been there a second before. Where had he come from?

The shaven-headed man turned right onto the sidewalk, going down the street ahead of us, but as I watched, I saw that the other man did not go into the building that he had turned toward before banging into the first man; rather, he walked around the side of the building for some unexplainable and abstract reason. It didn't seem like there were any entrances on the side of the building where he was walking.

The strange thing about this chance meeting between the two men was that there was plenty of room for a few dozen people to walk in the spot where they met, tons more room than what was needed for two men to walk without bumping into each other. Why did they brush up against each other and keep walking without saying a word? Neither of them seemed to act like they took any notice of this bizarre pedestrian crash. The episode was strikingly ridiculous, yet it appeared that neither of the men seemed to care about the odd way they banged into the other.

Only seconds later, as the same shaven-headed man continued up the empty sidewalk of the spacious street, he unexpectedly turned sharply left into the street in front of a parked car. At that exact second, a young man appeared on the sidewalk across the street from out of nowhere. This young man left the sidewalk and cut left so that he and the shaven-headed man banged up against each other in the middle of the empty street. They did not look at each other or say a word, but kept walking.

"What's going on here?" I asked Diane.

"What's wrong?" she asked.

"You didn't see what just happened?

"No," said Diane. "What happened?"

"You didn't see the two men collide into each other?"

"No."

I didn't know how Diane could have missed the event, because she was looking up the block and they were the only things moving on the street. As the light changed to green and we started to roll forward, I explained what I saw transpire between the shaven-headed man and the younger man in the street, and the similar event between the shaven-headed man and the man in front of the building.

"That man?" Diane asked, aiming her chin over the steering wheel at the shaven-headed man as he turned left around the corner and onto Wakefield Avenue and soon came to a halt in front of the bus stop for the N15 bus to Roosevelt Field Mall.

"Yes," I said, "that's him."

We came to the red light on the corner of Wakefield Avenue, so we had a minute to observe the shaven-headed man, who stood on the corner to our left. I noticed a white earphone in his right ear with a thin, white wire going down to a cell phone or some other device in his right hand.

"Maybe he's a cop," I said. "Maybe he and the other guys he bumped into are passing notes." But I hadn't seen any sort of exchange like that.

"Maybe they were passing drugs to each other," Diane said.

"I don't think so," I said. "I didn't see their hands pass anything. Hell, they didn't even look at each other."

Diane made a left onto Wakefield Avenue so we could observe the shaven-headed man better from a front view. He didn't see us pass directly in front of him on the road. If he was a cop, either he was a great faker in his efforts to act like he didn't see us observing him, or he was particularly unaware of his environment. His eyes were glued to his cell phone, but his mouth never moved;

therefore, he wasn't talking to anybody on the phone. Our next thought was that maybe what he was really doing was listening to someone give him instructions. Maybe he was receiving instructions about us.

Odd, I thought, *most people wear a set of headphones when they listen to music from a hand-held device. This guy has only one earphone in his right ear, like a federal agent listening to a walkie-talkie.*

In order to stay in the area, Diane had to make a right, and then another right, and then another right. Finally, we were back on Wakefield Avenue. Diane pulled her black Kia Soul over on the shoulder of the road in front of a store. We were now situated diagonally across the street from the corner bus stop so we could observe the shaven-headed man from a distance. We watched him and tried to figure out if he was a cop, perhaps involved in an investigation of someone, say a criminal or a terrorist in the area, or if he was a federal agent watching us, or whether he was a Man in Black following us. This was all getting mind-boggling and a little wearisome.

That's when the ugly, weathered, bearded face of an old man who had the blurred light blue eyes of a dead person appeared outside the passenger window. His ruddy face loomed before the glass like a deflated balloon. He was pushing a shopping cart in which rolled empty, dirty soda cans and beer bottles. He mouthed a few words into my window, asking me to roll down the window so he could address us. But Diane caught sight of him and immediately started the car. I always regretted not hearing what he had to say, for maybe he was a messenger. Maybe his words would have passed the meaning of the events I had witnessed involving the shaven-headed man. We'll never know.

"Oh, my god," Diane exclaimed, and she pulled her car away from the curb into the street, passing the shaven-headed man a last time on her way out of Lakeview.

23

Shadow Person interrupts lecture.

The next day, March 28, 2013, Diane and I spoke as *The Paranormal Adventurers* at Middle Country Public Library. This library has two branches: an older building in Selden and a newer facility in Centereach. On this occasion, we were speaking in the newer facility in Centereach.

The Centereach Library is large. We never had a problem with the electricity in the Community Room because the building is modern, with adequate power for anything that might be needed. Our equipment does not require much power, anyhow. We were using a PA system, a projector, and a laptop computer—barely any energy at all. But ten minutes before we were to begin speaking, the circuit breaker in the room blew. With a packed audience waiting for a show, this led to some stress for library staff, who set out to immediately solve the problem. A librarian got hold of the custodian, who in turn found that he could not solve the problem right then—because he was mystified.

"I never saw this happen here before," said the flustered custodian, scratching his head. "In all the years I worked at this library, I never once saw the power go."

As he moved further into the room, he paused and dread fell over his face. He looked like he had seen a ghost. He immediately rushed up to me and came close and with a serious, worried expression, informing me that when he looked at me from across the room, thinking how he could solve the strange electrical problem, he saw a black figure, like a shadow, dart across the room in front of him.

"It was like a thick shadow that ran away from me," he said seriously, his eyes full of wonder and maybe a little terror. "I saw this shadowy black thing move right in front of me!"

He then rushed to Diane to tell her the same story. The people sitting in the chairs waiting for the program to begin stared at the custodian with open mouths, because they'd heard him telling us about the shadow person. They looked afraid. To get through the program, we had to hook up our power strips to a few 100-foot long wires that led to a plug in another meeting room that had power.

I couldn't help but wonder if the black figure and the power outage were just some more strange signs that something not human was paying attention to us because of my calling of extraterrestrials in the graveyard on the night of the CE-5 meeting. After all, it might have been aliens that took out the power in the blackout of 1965.

CHAPTER SIX

2010
Long Island Devil
Investigation Revisited

24

Never documented.

As far as I knew at the time, the strange cryptid, the Long Island Devil, had never been documented. However, similar misfits of the paranormal have been seen in other places, including Baltimore, Maryland, in 1951, and in England several times, just to name a couple. Here on Long Island, I've never met anyone who has ever heard of a being, or anything, like the Long Island Devil. However, in 1880, the *New York Times* published a report that hundreds of people saw a man with wings and the legs of a frog flying through the air, about a thousand feet above Coney Island.

So, I contacted the people I wanted on the investigation team for the spring of 2010, and set up a date to meet in the parking lot of the Bethpage Public Library. It's a big municipal lot located across the street from the Bethpage Public Library building. I wanted to meet outside, so we could talk loudly and drink coffee and, if anybody wanted to smoke, they could do so freely.

On the given day in the spring, we met at six-thirty in the evening. People were coming from work in a constant stream from the nearby Long Island Railroad station and getting wearily into their cars in the parking lot, so they could get home to dinner and their families. They gave us odd stares, for clearly it was an unusual sight, seeing a large group of people in a big circle in the parking lot at dinnertime.

Just about everyone I had invited to the initial meeting showed up—about twenty-five people in all. One man who attended, a retired librarian on the

The Quaker Burial Ground in Farmingdale. This is the center cemetery of three strung together. The building on the site is an active Quaker Meeting House.

elderly side who was also a learned cryptozoologist with a doctorate from the University of Virginia, sat in a lawn chair because he had trouble standing. The day was mild, but cool. I had the people gather before me and I introduced Patrick Kenney and explained the situation. Everybody wanted in. We all got in our cars and took a ride to the spot where Kenney had seen the creature. There, Kenney explained what he saw so that the investigators could more clearly imagine the events connected to the sighting. From there we went to the graveyards down the block and inspected them, wondering if there was a connection to them as well.

These are actually three old graveyards strung together. The cemeteries are not big and most of the graves are old. Each cemetery has woods to one side or the other. Collectively, paranormalists call the graveyards The Old Quaker Burying Ground because the tiny center cemetery is an old burial ground for Quakers and, to this day, there is still an active Quaker meeting house on the property. In fact, the graveyards are strung together along a narrow road called Quaker Meeting House Road.

25

Implant?

One morning, not long after the 2013 CE-5 gathering in the haunted graveyard of Yaphank, I woke up, feeling exhausted. My fingers found a bump on my left shoulder. In the bathroom, I pulled a long, black item from the flesh of my left shoulder. It reminded me of one of the black cloves my mother used to stick into hams before baking them in the kitchen oven. The top of the item that I pulled out of my shoulder was round and broke in my fingers. I took a magnifying glass to it under a light; it seemed to be made of tiny fibers that looked like electronics. I immediately thought the item was a microchip of some sort. I wondered if it had been inserted into my flesh while I slept. If it had, it either had not yet worked itself into my body, or it might have been defective and did not settle the correct way into the skin. I stopped myself with this thinking, though, and looked at myself in the mirror, frowning at my own face, shaking my head at myself, realizing how absurd I was for thinking all these ludicrous thoughts.

The skin underneath the chip was not damaged, even though the tail on this thing was half an inch long. It slipped out of my flesh and skin without hurting or leaving an opening. It felt strange to witness this. It was like seeing someone throw a brick into a pond without seeing a splash. The skin was red, but there was no wound.

*

Notes to self:

The Anti-UFO Army helicopters chase the extraterrestrial crafts. It happened over my house in Rocky Point several times now.

I have bad dreams. I remember strange eyes. Not human eyes. Bug eyes. Wrap-around eyes. A black cat appears in my yard and often observes me. It has yellow eyes. It visits my property and is not afraid of me. It never comes close to me. It always seems to be around on a morning following dreams I have about the eyes. I realized one day, as I stared at the cat, staring at me without moving, that this was my "familiar." During the witchcraft trials in Salem, Massachusetts, in 1692, prosecutors attacked accused witches for having familiars, mostly cats. They were connected to the Devil. Now I wonder if familiars are like bugging devices that transmit information back to the spaceships and keep an eye on potential resistors to the alien invasion. Were the witchcraft trials really more about local girls meeting up with extraterrestrials than agents of the Devil? Am I growing insane?

*

On the afternoon of Sunday, April 7, 2013, Diane and I were in my house in Rocky Point discussing all these strange things that were happening to me, when we heard a tremendous crash and felt the ground rumble from something that was happening outside the house. When we ran outside to see what the matter was, we found a giant tree at the side of my yard had broken at its base and this massive tree, with all its heavy branches, had collapsed across the road with a mighty boom. The top of the tree was in someone else's yard, clear across the street. Not only did the tree collapse, it was so enormous that it pulled down all the wires strung between utility poles across the street and felled the wires clear down to the corner, where a fire was in progress from an arching electrical wire sparking dry leaves on the ground. The neighborhood was flooded with stinky blue smoke of rubber, tar, leaves, and grass. The arcing wire was so powerful it could not be observed straight-on for more than a second at a time because it was as strong and bright white to the eyes as the sun itself.

The police and fire department arrived. The cops cordoned off the area with yellow DO NOT CROSS tape and, after an hour or so, the arcing wire was conquered and the threat of fire burning down the wooden utility pole on the corner was extinguished. The electric company, LIPA, arrived and spent the day getting the neighborhood's electrical power restored. A large swath of the neighborhood was without power for many hours because the main line had come down under the weight of the gargantuan tree. The main power line was the wire that was on fire on the ground near the utility pole. Meanwhile, the tree lay across the road. This made it difficult for people living in the area to get to their homes. It wasn't until the evening that town workers cut up the tree and hauled the wood off and the road was reopened. It seemed like every time I tried to discuss with Diane the oddities taking place in my life of late, something happened to sidetrack us.

A lengthy note I had on my computer screen about some of the things that were happening to me was wiped clean from the computer. A few files related to my study of UFOs over Long Island were also gone—even though it had all been saved. The disk drive was basically fried.

*

Then, on Wednesday, April 10, 2013, I stopped to look out my front window, only to see an enormous flame reach up twenty or so feet into the air in someone's backyard in the neighborhood. I had seen a few fires over the years, and because I knew how dangerous they are, my heart raced upon seeing the leaping yellow and red flames. I was sure that this was a big fire—possibly the kitchen of somebody's home had exploded into flames.

As I stood there, in that brief second, deciding what I was going to do about the fire, I saw the flames suddenly subside and disappear. There was no smoke at all. I threw on my boots and ran down the block and peeked into the backyard where I saw this giant fire spring to life, but there was no sign a fire had ever been there. Nobody was outside. Had I dreamt what I saw?

Then I remembered the mega jumbo jet hanging motionless and silent in the sky over Garden City, and I wondered if the appearance of the fire was related to the illusion of the jet. Everything was starting to seem strange to me. Often now, one thing reminded me of another. Recent events that were unrelated seemed strangely related. I wondered if I was looking at things the way I suspected a madman might look at things, and I grew concerned for my mental health. Was I becoming insane, or was I observing what I was meant to observe by dictate of the aliens?

Were the aliens showing me secrets, or were they trying to drive me to the point of insanity? After all, insanity is a place from which nobody listens seriously to what you have to say about UFOs. Isn't that true? Remember John Ford? He's still in a psychiatric hospital. If you don't remember him, read on. I will remind you later. He's a supposed madman who many people regard as a hero because he warned us of the invasion three decades ago (see section 29).

*

Then, on Monday, April 22, 2013, I witnessed another motionless airplane hanging in the sky over Long Island. But this incident occurred during the daytime and in clear view of thousands of rush-hour commuters on the highway.

Not even two months had passed since I participated in the fateful CE-5 meeting at the back of Almshouse Cemetery in Yaphank. Only fifty-three days had elapsed since I saw an airplane hanging motionlessly and silently in the night sky over Garden City and instantaneously received a telepathic message that alien spaceships disguise themselves as airplanes so they can go about their business undetected by humans. These same two months were filled with bizarre happenings and inexplicable mysteries that didn't add up to anything concrete. I knew I was being shown little bits and fragments of a large tapestry, the whole of which I might never see, and thus I might never make sense of any of the little fragments that have come into play.

I spotted the white craft high up in the clear, blue sky while driving south on the Seaford-Oyster Bay Expressway (State Route 135), on my way to meet two

The old pine tree at Powell Cemetery. Is this where the alleged Long Island Devil takes cover when it visits the string of cemeteries in Bethpage known as the haunted Old Quaker Burying Ground?

A ladder of limbs and boughs may offer privacy to the alleged creature known as the Long Island Devil.

fellow paranormal investigators. The craft clearly looked like a jet. It was large, for sure. Initially, I didn't think much of the appearance of the plane, but as it stayed in my view and took center stage in the wide, powder-blue sky outside my windshield, there wasn't any way for me to avoid seeing it. As the seconds passed, I couldn't help but feel instinctively that the craft I was seeing was in the sky for my benefit, so I slowed the vehicle down and paid attention to it.

Incidentally, the two investigators who I was to meet that afternoon were brothers, burly fellows with big gray beards, who had their own personal takes on the paranormal. Diane and I had known Ralph and Dennis for years, and we stayed in touch through e-mail, though we rarely saw them. They were now to accompany me in a graveyard in Bethpage in search for signs of the presence of the Long Island Devil. It was the first time they'd ever be in that string of cemeteries.

On the passenger seat of my SUV was a pound of fresh Boar's Head liverwurst, which I would later smear all over the rough chunky bark of the trunk of the largest tree in haunted Powell Cemetery, the last cemetery in the line of three at Quaker Burying Ground. It was a monstrous old pine tree with endless thick boughs climbing up to dark mystery, providing lurid shade and cover for anything that would care to hide in it, and long shaggy branches of spiky, green needles and pine combs that a creature could climb down to snatch something up off the ground and then climb back up to hide, so it could eat its bounty in peace.

If the Long Island Devil was a carnivore, a meat eater, perhaps he'd smell the stinky liverwurst and appear. Of course, that was unlikely. More likely, if the Devil regularly visits the cemetery, perhaps it would smell this food and visit the base of that old pine tree more often on its rounds, just to see if there was any food planted there to eat. After all, the first time witness Patrick Kenney saw the cryptid, in 2008, in residential Farmingdale, it was lurched forward on a limb high up in a tree and pointing down at people having a springtime picnic or barbeque in a backyard. What a sight that must have been, a midnight black creature with wings and long bony black fingers, dressed in a cape and hood, standing thirty feet up in a tree pointing at humans—before it disappeared into thin air. Maybe it wanted the food the people were eating. Perhaps, every time I visited the cemetery and smeared liverwurst on the tree, the beast of Farmingdale and Bethpage would come looking for food and leave signs of its visits—foot prints, scat, urine, alien pictograms, holograms, mathematical formulas etched into the tree bark. Who knows? I had to try something!

Powell Cemetery is the prettiest of the three small cemeteries. It's pretty because its grounds are filled with old trees and lush, green grass. As mentioned, the three haunted graveyards are linked together on Quaker Meeting House Road in Bethpage. They are located directly across the narrow street from the entrance to Bethpage State Park Golf Course. The park features 1, 400 acres of greenery. I hypothesize that the park is probably where the Long Island Devil dwells, hiding in the tree tops or disguising itself as a large tree tumor, and only moves to unfold itself when night has settled in or when its hungry. Of course, if it can achieve invisibility, it can move about as it wishes. At its disposal are thousands of acres of additional greenery that are located to the north of Bethpage State Park that may offer more hiding spots for an elusive monster or lone extraterrestrial. (You might recall that Quaker Burying Ground is the very place where the inconclusive Long Island Devil Investigation took place in 2010.)

The experience I had on this day, in 2013, that I wish to share, started when I spotted a white airplane in the sky shortly after I got on the busy Seaford-Oyster Bay Expressway from the Long Island Expressway. The airplane was high up. As I continued driving, I noticed the airplane was not moving. For a minute I thought this was an optical illusion, but a raw excitement overtook me because, as the minutes went by, I realized this was not an airplane at all, but a silver disk that was stationary in the sky. I was certain that its appearance was for my education. Most likely, nobody but me even noticed it.

I drove extra slowly so I could watch the silver disk in the sky, much to the chagrin of the drivers behind me. At one point, I thought of pulling over to the shoulder of the highway to spy the craft, photograph it, and video record it, but the shoulder of the Seaford-Oyster Bay Expressway is a dangerous place to pull over. So, I continued on, getting off at the Exit 8 for Bethpage.

It was when I came to a halt at the stop sign at the end of the exit ramp that I saw that the airplane—or the alien craft—had disappeared from the sky. I craned my head all around to find it, but it was gone. The woman at the stop sign in front of me looked at her face in the mirror and touched her nose. Either she had not seen the craft in the sky, or she only saw a common airplane and her interest in the matter was nil.

Now I knew for certain that my first sighting of the airplane hanging silently in the sky over Garden City on the night I called aliens to Earth was not a misperception on my part, but that it actually happened. I was thankful for a second sighting of the phenomenon because it validated my first experience. UFOs are in the sky over Long Island, and I could see them.

26

I'm being hunted by UFOs.

All this, I present to you, dear reader, just for starters. It might all sound too crazy to be real, but it's all true!

As you can probably guess, I'm telling you about all these matters because pursuing the truth about spaceships over Long Island has become my life now. I ended up smack dab in the thick of it all when the truth became self-evident back in 1989, because I was a newspaper reporter in search of answers to questions about dead animals on an East End farm. Somehow it started there, but remained dormant, at least in my consciousness, till 2013, when I called the spaceships down with other UFO enthusiasts in the graveyard of Yaphank.

I don't know if you're supposed to call me a "UFO Contactee" or an "Extraterrestrial Hunter." I'll tell you, the way it really feels is I'm being hunted by UFOs, not the other way around. I suspect space aliens come in the middle of the night to people for their own reasons, without explaining anything to anyone. I was starting to wonder if they had come to me while I slept, too.

Where are they from? How long have they been watching us? How long have they been tagging unsuspecting humans with their microchip trackers? How many of us do they track?

Could there be millions of Contactees worldwide? Could there be billions of Contactees? Are there countless generations of families that have been tracked since the days Homosapiens first walked off the African plain to find new sources of food and firewood?

Note to Reader:

Now ask yourself a question: Are you reading this book because you're a Contactee? You should answer this question to yourself right now. Do you have strange dreams that involve creatures with big eyes? Have you ever woken up in a place you don't remember getting to? Have paranormal events taken place around you all your life? Has a shadow person ever appeared to you or around you? If you did see one, did it look like an Insectoid—an alien that is tall, slim, and all black, possibly like The Long Island Devil? Look up Insectoid on the Internet to see what people are saying about them. See drawings of them. Get to know what they are about. And look into Grays on the Internet while you're at it. From what others have said, the Grays are the technicians.

I'll never forget the story a fellow worker told me in late August 2013, as we drove together through Southold with a van filled with residents from the Ridge House where we both worked. This woman told me the following story and I never saw her again because she quit the next day. Let's call her Zoey.

Zoey said she grew up in Plainview. When she was seven, she found herself waking up in bed fully dressed in clothing that she had not put on, she said. Her mother was startled upon seeing her.

"Zoey," her mother cried. "Why are you dressed like that? Who dressed you?"

She asked this question because the clothing Zoey was wearing was intricate and her mother knew Zoey would not have been able to pick out these clothes and put them on all by herself.

"I don't know," Zoey said. "I didn't put them on. *They* put them on me."

"Who are *they?*" asked her mother.

"Zoey pointed upwards, "I don't know," she said. "*They* brought me someplace, but I can't remember where."

Her mother recoiled.

When I asked Zoey who she believed they were, she said: Grays. She told me she believes alien Grays entered her room, dressed her, and brought her to a spaceship and examined her. She said she now has dreams almost every night of ghosts, or something else that talks to her, showing her things, but she can't remember what she is being shown.

"My family makes fun of me because of the people I see in my dreams. They scare me. I wake up screaming. I have problems falling asleep. I'm afraid to close my eyes and dream."

Zoey told me all this without knowing anything about my involvement with UFOs and alien beings.

27

Insectoids and Grays.

I now spend much of my time searching the Internet for reports of Insectoids and Grays visiting Long Islanders in the middle of the night, and for reports of a strange creature (the Long Island Devil), and, of course, spaceships seen over the Pine Barrens. It's extremely time-consuming to do this. People don't want what they tell me to go on record. They tell me things because they just have to unload their experiences to someone, and they know their friends and family members won't understand; they're afraid they'll be labeled nuts.

I'm forever in pursuit of the elusive Long Island Devil of Farmingdale and Bethpage, and I won't give up, because it might be an Insectoid that is roaming the trees, waiting to be saved by its own kind. I believe the all-black creature seen in residential neighborhoods and woods is an extraterrestrial that either survived being shot down in an alien craft over Moriches Bay, in 1989, by a military jet or helicopter belonging to the Anti-UFO Army, or it's a survivor of a spaceship crash in Southaven Park from 1992.

If confronted face-to-face, would the Long Island Devil, a beast most likely possessing wings and an elongated alien-shaped head with a larger then human brain in it, have answers for us that could explain where the extraterrestrials stalking our neighborhoods come from in our Milky Way Galaxy? There are more than 400,000,000,000 stars in our galaxy. Some scientists say there might be even a trillion galaxies. There are literally billions of solar systems out there, potentially tens of billions of planets in our galaxy alone, many of which might support intelligent civilizations that are much more advanced than our own. In fact, as of November 4, 2013, NASA's Kepler spacecraft, launched in 2009, discovered over 3,500 candidate alien worlds, with 104 planets in habitable zones. And that's only in our local neighborhood of stars. Scientists say there are tens of billions of possibly habitable planets in the Milky Way Galaxy, with as many as 6,000,000,000,000,000,000,000 *sextillion* planets in the visible universe, many of which could be habitable. From where do the aliens that visit Earth come? A bigger question is how did they get here? The biggest question is now that they're here, what are they going to do?

Maybe the aliens currently studying Earth are not from our galaxy, but from a galaxy a million light years away. Are they even from our universe? Could they be from a universe that can only be reached through dimensions we can't access or even conceive of at this time? Did they master wormholing through time and space?

Whatever the aliens are about, and wherever they come from, mine is not a life I would have chosen when I left the State University of New York at Stony Brook, in 1981, as a bright and shiny English major with a minor in history to start my happy life as a full-fledged adult and tax-paying member of society. Nonetheless, a Contactee and UFO Hunter is now the life I live.

PART III

CHAPTER SEVEN

UFOS OVER THE PINE BARRENS

28

What's at stake?

Sign on Route 27 (Sunrise Highway) in Manorville announces the densest region of Pine Barrens on Long Island.

Many of the stories I wrote back in 1989 were about the ancient Pine Barrens forest of Long Island. Back then, before the New York State Assembly passed the Long Island Pine Barrens Preservation Act on July 4, 1993, and Governor Mario Cuomo signed the legislation into law, everybody with money in their pockets was rushing to build or invest in massive condominium projects in the ecologically sensitive Pine Barrens forest located in eastern Long Island. All the builders wanted their plans to be "grandfathered in" before the state's environment laws got too rigid for builders to do what they wanted, analogous to cowboys in the old West shooting up the town on Saturday nights. They knew a change in the law regarding the Pine Barrens was coming. Because of the Preservation Act, today the Pine Barrens are noted not for elaborate condominium developments, but for the beauty of the land in its natural state.

Since the days of the Indians, this area of Long Island has been known as a hotbed of paranormal activity, especially ghosts and UFOs, though there are those, such as Nicholas Voulgaris of Levittown, MUFON's Chief Field Investigator in New York State, who say that Long Island is not a hotbed, but just another place where UFOs are seen, like any other place. In an interview, Nick said in the months just prior to the writing of this book, that most activity on Long Island occurred along the north shore. He said some of the incidents involved helicopters chasing UFOs. He added that he has met people in his five years as a MUFON Field Investigator who claim there is a an opening or tear in space above the Long Island Sound and through this opening spaceships come to Earth. Nick did not personally support or oppose this belief.

I'd like to think that, back in 1989, I had something to do with educating people about waves of spaceships visiting Long Island; but the truth is, I was on the other side of the fence. I was like an ostrich with my head buried in the sand. And I wasn't alone, either. The Police, the Distinct Attorney, the politicians, and the public at large were right there beside me with their heads in the sand, ignoring a problem to which we should have been paying our full attention because the fate of all... well, humanity could ultimately be at stake.

29

John Ford.

No, my story begins back when people much braver than me led the fight to tell the world what was really going on with the alien invasion of Long Island and America—indeed, the world. It seemed nobody was noticing what was happening right under their noses, except UFO researchers and those who actually experienced close encounters—and the Anti-UFO Army, of course. Maybe nobody else wanted to notice. I can't blame people for wanting to avoid the truth in this awful case. I almost wish I could go back in time or discard from my memory all the things that happened to me and details that I have learned about extraterrestrials.

As of this writing, one of the leaders for the cause for human freedom from alien slavery, John Ford, is still in an upstate New York State psychiatric hospital on the Hudson. He's a prisoner at Mid-Hudson Forensic Psychiatric Center, a maximum security New York State facility of cold brick and steel in New Hampton, not far from Bear Mountain and West Point. In 1996, he was arrested for conspiracy to commit murder and other charges along with another man, who later served five and a half years in prison. Ford's belief in UFOs was at the heart of his legal problems.

The court deemed Ford incompetent to stand trial for the array of charges brought against him, saying he was delusional.

"They thought I was delusional because I believed in UFOs," Ford told me and Diane from across a table in the drab visitors' canteen at the hospital on October 19, 2013, where we went to visit him after corresponding by U.S. mail for some time. "A judge recently took that off the list against me," Ford added, "because he said everybody believes in UFOs."

Ford went on, "And they said I was a paranoid schizophrenic because I said I was recruited by the CIA when I got out of college, so I could report on the activities of KGB agents. The judge scratched that off the list, too, saying I'm not paranoid or a schizophrenic for saying that."

Ford hopes these changes to his profile will soon result in him being moved to a civil hospital, where he will enjoy freedoms he does not now enjoy. He is very hopeful that before that could even happen he will be set free sometime in early 2014 as the result of a trial based on an appeal. He blames his old lawyer for not doing his job right by telling Ford to take a plea that landed him in the hospital for so long: 17 years.

I prefer to believe that when John Ford first started the Resistance to alien tyranny by spreading the word of the invasion of Long Island, that he was completely sane and on a mission from which he got detained by the authorities who wanted him silenced. Maybe the aliens planted it in his head that he was an unpaid CIA spy whose work was so secretive that his name could not be listed on CIA records and would thus never receive any pay. I wouldn't put it past them.

My hypothesis is extraterrestrials send humans behavior-altering messages in the waves through electronics, possibly through mysterious high intensity flashes of light and/or sounds that trigger desired responses. Perhaps we are not advanced enough to understand how these light flashes and sounds carry such messages. Or, maybe, the chips the aliens plant in people's bodies carry sets of instructions that are uploaded when triggered by the above means.

Transmissions we can't even hear might be sent every minute over the wires entering our homes, inaudible voices speaking to us through the handsome digital televisions in our bedrooms at night as we drift off to sleep, and talking to us when we first wake up to a clock radio tuned to our favorite station in the morning. Could it be that we listen to the silent instructions as we drive to work, and when we hear music in elevators and in restaurants at lunchtime? It's my personal theory that these triggers could set in motion behaviors according to instructions we were told to obey, possibly first when the aliens came to see us personally in our bedrooms, or in some cases, when they beamed us up to their spaceships for exams. These little trips we might take from cars or while we walk our dogs are hidden in our subconscious, like files that we put at the back of the cabinet to forget. It's my belief the instructions they feed us benefit them, not us.

At any rate, Ford, an unmarried Bellport resident who worked as a Suffolk County Court officer until he retired, and who lived with his mother at the time of his arrest, was founder and chairman of the Long Island UFO Network (LIUFON). The organization was made an incorporated entity in 1988 after six months or so of existence as an association, Ford told me. He said his interest in UFOs began when he and his mother witnessed a UFO in the skies in 1981.

"It had energy around it, pulsing, and then it just shot right off!" His hand went straight up in the air as he said this: "A ninety-degree angle." He calls Long Island, "A hotbed of UFO activity."

Ford was sent to the state psychiatric hospital as a prisoner after he was arrested for allegedly plotting to kill three political figures from Suffolk County. James Catterson, the Suffolk County District Attorney at the time, said Ford planned to kill these certain influential political figures because he perceived them opposing his message to the public about the coming of the spaceships and about a UFO cover-up.

Among other things, Ford blamed the politicians he was accused of plotting to murder for causing a large fire that raged in the Pine Barrens of Suffolk County in 1995. He insisted that the fires were purposely set to cover up a spaceship crash in Riverhead, near Suffolk Community College. He said in order to hide evidence of the crash, committeemen from the Republican Party in Suffolk County started fires in the Pine Barrens to divert attention away from the fire the spaceship caused. According to Ford, the thinking was that if the woods all around the community college were set afire, nobody would focus on the UFO fire, and authorities would have time to clean up the debris, hiding the evidence.

Ford asserted that the alleged intentionally set fires, which ate thousands of acres of trees, had a second advantage for local politicians who saw a way to sell county land cheaply to friends and make some money for themselves on the side.

District Attorney Catterson, a tough white-haired, snub-nosed detective type, who I interviewed for newspapers and on television many times before Ford was arrested, held press conferences in which he said Ford planned to kill these people by covertly inserting radioactive radium in their toothpaste and by spreading the radioactive hot material on their car door handles. Reportedly, Ford was illegally in possession of radium stolen from the Grumman plant in Bethpage by Ford's friend "who just took it," Ford told me and Diane.

Ford quoted his friend: "'I got some radium and I don't know what to do with it.' Well, I had three Geiger counters. I said I'd take the radium to use it to calibrate my Geiger counters."

When asked how much radium his friend gave him, Ford said it was a small glob of the material that could easily fit into the very center of one's palm. "Grumman told the police it was just low-grade stuff used for instruments, like clocks. But when they had Brookhaven National Lab look at it, the Lab said, 'Woe, this stuff is dangerous!' But it wasn't. They were exaggerating. The District Attorney ran with it."

Catterson acknowledged, at the time, that in order to kill people, Ford would have had to insert radium in the toothpaste tubes of his victims for more than twenty years, maybe even more like forty years. Even with obvious contradictions about how dangerous Ford really was at the time, it seemed everyone thought he was nuts—including me.

Obviously, after considering it, any thinking person would have to ask how Ford could have possibly slipped into a politician's home—week after week—to insert radium into fresh tubes of toothpaste without being noticed? And in order to do that, Ford would have had to have a lot more radium than was in his possession. Indeed, how could Ford have even considered pulling off such a strategically impossible feat? Were the charges against him exaggerated? Did the District Attorney's office make the case a lot beefier than it really was? Ford certainly thinks so.

Many Long Islanders, like me, now believe the case against John Ford was ludicrous and largely fabricated. While it was believed he was a terrorist who was out to kill government leaders, he was no terrorist. The thirty-five handguns and rifles he had in his home were a personal collection, he said.

We know from court hearings that authorities believed Ford was going to try to kill the political figures via an informant who was wearing a wire and whose questions led Ford to talk of inserting radium into the politicians' toothpaste. Ford maintained that he was only joking with the informant at the time he was recorded talking about inserting radium in their toothpaste and truly never intended to kill or hurt anybody. The recordings of the discussion between Ford and the informant were murky and hard to hear clearly. These days, Ford maintains he has proof the tape that was recorded of him talking with the wired informant was edited twenty-one times by the District Attorney's office to be made more damaging against him. He plans to use this information about the editing of the tape, in addition to claims that his search warrant was illegal, to be set free by a judge when he appeals his indictment sometime in 2014.

While Ford obviously was involved in illegal activities, there are those of us who believe John Ford was militant on behalf of Long Island residents. In many people's eyes, he was a hero because he was telling everyone the truth about the UFO invasion, though perhaps muddled in his own personality. In this case, the truth did not set him free—it landed him in jail for seventeen years with the possibility of many more to come.

In fact, Ford's case is the first and only case in the nation of a Ufologist prosecuted for crimes related to his beliefs about spaceships and a government cover-up. The evidence against him, many people believe, was conjured through entrapment and fabrications. Some people, who support Ford, and even Ford himself, maintain he was put away because he was getting too close to exposing widespread corruption in the Brookhaven Town and Suffolk County governments. In fact, one of the men he allegedly planned to kill was later arrested and spent two years in prison for corruption related to involvement in a chop shop in Patchogue and for allegedly taking bribes for allowing illegal dumping in the town's landfill in Medford.

It's my opinion John Ford was taken off the streets for speaking out publicly about Long Island's plague of UFOs. It is pure folly to believe Ford had such preposterous assassinations planned for the three political figures involving toothpaste poisonings. Unless he was from Mars himself, he could not have possibly believed he could have carried out a prolonged attack against his perceived enemies through radioactive radium death rays. He wasn't an idiot. And he's still not.

According to the website for the psychiatric hospital where Ford is held:

> MHFPC is a secure adult psychiatric center that provides a comprehensive program of evaluation, treatment, and rehabilitation for patients admitted by court order. These admissions are consequent to judicial findings of "incompetent to stand trial" or "not responsible by reason of mental disease or defect."
> www.omh.ny.gov/omhweb/facilities/mhpc/facility.htm

What a perfect way to get someone off the streets without even a trial! These days, Ford spends much of his time in the hospital reading: "Books about UFOs," he says. There's not much in terms of activities there for him, and there are no field trips, he adds. He has no Internet access, and friends come to visit only once every four months or so. Once every month patients are allowed to order food from an outside source, and this is typically the highlight of life at the facility. We brought him Chinese food for lunch when we visited.

He speaks calmly. "I am a patient man," he says. "I rely on my faith."

John Ford was silenced and subsequently LIUFON was given a death sentence. For LIUFON, it was a quick demise caused by fear and paralysis. Discussion of UFOs was virtually absent on Long Island afterwards; the public's interest seemed to die with LIUFON. Opposition to aliens and resistance to their forsaken agendas fell dead as a doornail with John Ford's arrest. The question is: how had the police and the DA's office been duped into believing this poppycock, too, and prosecuting Ford for it? How could they prosecute a man for such a ridiculous plan?

One could argue that it wasn't the cops', District Attorney's, or politicians' fault that they went after Ford. Maybe they were only doing what the aliens instructed them to do to shut Ford up.

"It's my belief the Grays are not our friends," said Ford, sitting stoically in a chair in the canteen of twelve tables fixed immovably to the ground. He wears a gray beard and a gray sweater. His hands are folded passively on the table. Officers are watching us from across the room. Outside the windows of the canteen, rolls of barbed wire shine in the afternoon autumn sunlight at the top of twenty-foot tall fences, keeping prisoners' hopes from ever getting out by their own efforts down to zero. "The aliens don't care about us. They want our DNA. That's why they're here. They need our genetic material to strengthen themselves. I believe they will soon be making themselves known to us. They will tell us who they are and show themselves."

30

Hypothetical example of alien mind control.

Let's take one hypothetical example of alien mind control: that would be gold.

Why do we value gold so highly? Why do we pool it together in nice, heavy gold bars at the Federal Reserve building in Manhattan? Could it be that gold is an item of particular importance to space creatures because it is the best conductor of electricity and resists rust unlike other metals? Could it be the aliens told us to worship, mine, and protect gold and develop a monetary system based on it, so that we will continue to seek it out of mountainsides, to mine it, even worship it in the form of a golden calf? Could this have first started in Mesopotamia many thousands of years ago? Will, one day, the aliens come to the secure gold installations of the world, like Fort Knox and the Federal Reserve Building, to collect all the gold that we accumulated like honey for the beekeepers? Would they be off and on their way only to show up again a few hundred years into the future to collect more?

Aliens might be able to send us instructions and messages through televisions, radios, sounds, and light. In addition, it is well established by abductees that space visitors send messages and instructions directly through telepathy. That's how they got me in Garden City that night in 2013, when a spaceship appeared in the sky, enormous and close up. I immediately got rid of my telephone, cable television, and Internet service, and I never listen to the radio any more. I take note of bright flashes of light that seem to come out of nowhere, too. Of course, I still have to use telephones and computers with Internet service, but I limit my usage to that which is necessary. I hope I am being overly cautious because I don't want to believe space visitors are really controlling us through modern technologies.

31

Aliens and Men in Black.

Of course, by now, I, like so many others I am meeting, am so deep into alien contact that I may never find a way out. I'm a reluctant Contactee. Then there are those like Lilly, who I met at a MUFON meeting: she does not fight them. Initially, they reached me telepathically, but every day they remind me they are watching. I see their Men in Black following me, and government Anti-UFO Army agents that are always somewhere present watching the Men in Black. I see the spaceships and Anti-UFO Army jets and helicopters following the spaceships.

If the aliens contact you, they as good as own you unless you resist; and even though you realize they got you, and even though you resist, as I do, they still have your mind the way they want it. However, there is still some wiggle room, because they do not dominate the entire mind of a human. Human resistance means nothing to these beings, so they pay little attention to that side of us, it seems; but they underestimate our ability to fight back. To them, whatever we feel or may have to say in resistance is insignificant and has no effect on their agendas. Resisting is equivalent to ants telling us in ant language that they don't want us running our lawn mowers over their holes anymore because it bothers them and often kills them.

We don't know who they are, or where they're from, or how they were able to figure out how to bend time and space to shoot light years across the heavens, from one end of our galaxy, or the known universe, to the other. We only know they're out there, watching, studying us—like specimens in glass tanks like the alien-human babies Janet Russell (see section 34) saw inside their spaceships when she was abducted—and making decisions for Humankind that we can't even suspect. If the government knows what the aliens want and where they're from, they're not saying. That's most likely because the news would be too frightening and depressing for us to want to know.

Though we may not see insignias on their uniforms, the government has unleashed a powerful team of Anti-UFO agents to go after these aliens, and they are tireless. In an age when our government is met with cynicism and apathy, I say we should support the United States of America's government with all we have, because America is the only government out there that is probably fighting the extraterrestrials to get them off our planet. Let's just hope they know how to do it; the rest of us certainly don't.

32

Spreading the word.

Everything is different for me today compared to back in 1989 when all this started with a simple phone call from a woman who wanted me to go look at a pond located in Southaven County Park in Shirley, where she discovered dead bullfrogs by the dozens (see section 43). This is the same park where Governor Mario Cuomo signed the Pine Barrens Preservation Act back in July, 1993, preserving over 100,000 acres of Pine Barrens from sprawling overdevelopment.

These days, in addition to books, I also write for the national publication *FATE* magazine. It's a magazine dedicated to the study of the paranormal. Diane and I wrote a lengthy story about UFOs invading Long Island, which *FATE* informed me they will be publishing in a "Special UFO Issue," supporting Long Islanders in their Resistance by broadcasting the news of the invasion. *FATE* also published other stories of ours related to UFOs and the search for the Long Island Devil. This magazine has been around since 1948 and is one of the leading magazines of its type in America. It was in an article in *FATE* where the term "flying saucer" first appeared in a public forum in *FATE's* first year of publication.

I write about aliens on Long Island so people know what's going to happen to us in the future unless something changes, which is unlikely, unless the Anti-UFO Army can do something to get the Grays and Insectoids out of our skies and off our planet. It might be like spitting into the wind, but I'm doing what I can with my skills. My greatest hope is that if we can't get rid of them, that we can convince them to respect the sanctity of human life, and to help us develop new life-saving technologies and provide information about the cosmos and other species that live on other planets.

33

Recap. And a look at ghosts and Bigfoot.

My investigations partner Diane Hill has a keen mind and a sharp tongue. We've been around the paranormal bush many times and experienced many of the things you might think of when it comes to ghosts, haunting spirits, and the Unknown. Now, as you have read, we're aiming ourselves at the UFO problem. Diane is aware that I'm being watched and followed. One of the regular problems I have is that helicopters circle my house at all hours of the day and night, nearly every day, it seems. She didn't believe me until she witnessed a helicopter shining its bright searchlight into my windows on that late night of August 10, 2013. They usually stay up high, but sometimes they come down and the occupants stare at my house.

The government agents are watching me; or rather, they are watching the creatures who are watching me. I have seen the helicopters above my house with their powerful search lights on my roof and in my windows, only to suddenly rush off with the lights tilted up at something flying above them in the night.

A field investigator will never run out of paranormal occurrences on Long Island. This island, jutting out into the cold Atlantic Ocean the way it does, like a nervous whale that wants to swim away from the mainland, is endlessly haunted and obviously plagued by spaceships. Some Long Islanders are embarrassed about the high level of paranormal activity occurring in their quaint hometowns where whale-hunting was once a viable trade. Many Long Islanders act like it's a big secret that paranormal things are happening under our noses and we're powerless to do anything about it. Some people are angry that things are so out of kilter here compared to the rest of America. Any Long Islander with half a brain knows what's going on because it's all over YouTube in the form of videos showing UFOs flying over our homes and bays.

One video on YouTube shows objects over Lake Ronkonkoma: http://www.youtube.com/watch?v=q8Be1MV1_l8.

Another video exhibits a UFO over Wainscott, on eastern Long Island: http://www.youtube.com/watch?v=mzNyEUikNuo.

Yet another shows strange lights over the Atlantic Ocean as seen from the island city of Long Beach: http://www.youtube.com/watch?v=BppokMp6EFk.

There are many others.

That's where Diane and I come in. We're searching for answers and we're digging for information. Our goal these days is to uncover the truth and extent of the alien invasion and learn how we can do something about it.

A crop of one of Daniel Marquardt's seventeen photos of a UFO over Jones Beach shows a whitish–blue object with a red object above. In other photos he took, the red object is much closer to the white one. Mr. Marquardt said it looked like it was some kind of laser beam being emitted from the white object.

Of course, to understand the extent of the UFO infiltration, everyone from government leaders down to the homeless man on the street has to contribute knowledge of what he or she has seen in the skies over Long Island, and of the crafts and beings that have sometimes been seen landing on the ground. Abductees and Contactees have to bring forth any useful information about how to communicate effectively with them and how to defeat them. Before that even happens, we have to admit there are ghosts and UFOs on Long Island in a disproportionate number to the rest of America and to the rest of the world, and that ghosts and aliens might even be tied together, that in many cases they might even be the same thing. The Long Island Devil is a prime example. There are many people who think it's a ghost.

Ghosts tend to appear more commonly in areas where UFOs are known to appear, as if some opening to the paranormal had been torn open. Long Island is a paranormal hotspot of the first degree when it comes to both.

In the summer of 2013, Nassau Community College Professor Ted Benitt delivered a lecture to MUFON, in which he said Bigfoot are often associated with the appearances of UFOs. He said witnesses have claimed spaceships are seen in the skies over areas where Bigfoot are spotted, and that Bigfoot display the ability to disappear and teleport themselves to different places.

In fact, Diane and I would take the UFO problem over Long Island a step farther. We'd say Long Island is a microcosm of things to come for the rest of the United States and for the entire world.

The spaceships are coming. There is no doubt. This is not so much a prediction as a realization for Long Islanders. UFOs are in our skies today. I've seen them and so have thousands of other Long Islanders. As many scientists and researchers insist, our face-to-face introduction to space beings from other planets or other dimensions is at hand. Extraterrestrials have probably been here for thousands of years. We have become more aware of them within the last sixty years, since the day a spaceship crashed in the desert of Roswell, New Mexico, in 1947, and was subsequently covered up with stories about a weather balloon being recovered at the site—not a spaceship.

Some people believe aliens might have even had a hand in boosting our intelligence by blending their DNA with our own, as Long Island psychic Janet Russell believes. As mentioned, she claims she was abducted in 1962 while driving on Route 112 in Medford. She was apparently shown fetuses of hybrid humans and aliens in glass jars on a spaceship.

Unless we can stop them, it's possible we'll all have stories like Ms. Russell's to tell pretty soon.

34

A Case of abduction and missing time.

Here's Janet Russell's story, gathered from personal interviews and an essay Ms. Russell wrote that was originally printed in the December 16th edition of *The Press of Center Moriches*:

"I was pregnant with my daughter at the time," remembered Janet Russell.

"In 1962, I was twenty-two years-old and four-and-a-half months pregnant with my youngest child. I was on the way to the doctor for my monthly check up. I left the house at 6 p.m.

My appointment was scheduled for 6:15. The office wasn't far, so I knew I'd be there on time.

"As I was driving to the doctor's office on a well traveled road, Route 112 in Medford, I happened to glance up at the sky and saw something that looked like the moon. It was bigger than the moon and was purple. I remembered pulling over to get a better look at it. Just then, the purple moon faded away and became another color. It went from purple to blue to green to orange to silver. It looked like it was sequined and just kept spinning and fading out.

"Well, the next thing I knew I was at the doctor's office and it wasn't 6:15 p.m. It was 7:30 p.m. They were getting ready to close!

"The doctor asked me, 'Where have you been? You're usually so prompt!'

"I looked at him. 'What are you talking about?' I had no idea that I had lost over an hour's time.

"He asked, 'Were you in Florida?'

"I said, 'No, why?' It was March. Well, I saw in the mirror my face was so sunburned, it was actually peeling!"

Psychic Janet Russell in a graveyard at night. The frame is from a movie made by *The Paranormal Adventurers* that was aired on Ms. Russell's public access television show, *Beyond The Unexplained*. Ms. Russell had just finished saying that she was sure as she walked around the graveyard that the aliens that abducted her in 1962 were watching her from above.

Now, in her mid-70s, Ms. Russell can recall the details of her abduction by alien beings.

She believes she was brought into a spaceship by extraterrestrials and a chip was implanted into her right arm. With the help of hypnosis conducted by Dr. Jean Mundy, whom Ms. Russell said worked with abduction researcher Budd Hopkins, Ms. Russell was regressed to that day when she lost time while driving to the doctor's office. She recalled being ushered around the spaceship by Grays, a Nordic, a reptilian creature, and a being that looked like a praying mantis. She was brought into rooms and shown hybrid babies of humans and aliens growing in material that looked like the clear jelly in petri dishes.

"I think the chip they put in me is a tracking device," said Ms. Russell. "My daughter—the one I was pregnant with when I was abducted—also has the same scoop mark and a chip in her leg. I had an MRI taken of my arm. In it, you can see what looks like little electronics. The doctor said it looked like a bug bite that had calcified, but that it was no bug bite."

Ms. Russell said she never had the chip in her arm removed because she instinctively feels it would just grow back or burrow deeper. She could not fully explain her reluctance to me. Perhaps she was instructed by the aliens to not have it removed, and is thus obeying what she was told.

"I think the aliens are on Long Island because of the water around us," said Ms. Russell. "It's like the Bermuda Triangle. The crafts are submerged in the ocean, hiding from our view."

Ms. Russell believes aliens are visiting Earth to create hybrid humans by breeding humans with aliens in spaceship laboratories like the ones she saw on the alien craft. She also believes extraterrestrials breed with humans through in vitro fertilization.

"Think about it," Ms. Russell argued passionately, "fifty years ago, we didn't have the technology we have today. Thousands and thousands of years go by and suddenly within the span of fifty years we have color televisions, computers, microwaves, in vitro fertilization, MRIs, and many new and fantastic medicines. We are advancing quickly with their help."

But Ms. Russell can not say with any certainty why the aliens would want to help humans develop better technologies.

35

Small silver spacecraft lands.

Tall Al Gallant, on the other hand, now deceased, often retold his story of a small silver spacecraft he saw land in a sandy area beside a creek in Oceanside, Long Island, in the mid-1960s.

"It was a clear, bright day," Mr. Gallant would so often start his incredible tale. "I was a younger man back then. I was walking my dog, Barney, at the time."

Mr. Gallant, a tall, lanky man who lived and died alone in a gray apartment above a now long-bygone greasy luncheonette at the center of Oceanside, was generally regarded by the locals as eccentric because he often walked the streets with his little yellow dog, telling his story of a spaceship and extraterrestrials to anybody who would listen.

He'd spread his arms and raise his eyebrows: "I watched these two skinny little gray men get out of this shimmering silver disc that was only about fifteen feet in diameter," he would say. "It had red, green, and white lights that pulsated all around at different times. These little men looked at the creek and at the trees for a minute and then turned to me and my dog. They seemed to float—just float—without any effort at all!

"They came toward me and picked me up by the elbows and, the next thing I knew, the little men were getting back inside the silver disc and my dog and I were just standing there not knowing what had just happened to us. An hour had passed since we first saw them. But it seemed like seconds. What had they done with us in the hour that I could not account for?

"Then the disc just shot off, but with no sound," Mr. Gallant would continue. "It was gone in an instant. The ground where the disc landed was burnt with circles. The circles had three odd markings where the craft's supports sank into the sand."

According to Mr. Gallant, he and Barney then ran to the blue and white police booth in the center of Oceanside, where he told officers with guns his unbelievable story; but the officers only made fun of him and bullied him around, telling him to go home and "sleep it off," though he had not drunk any alcohol or taken any drugs, he said.

"Everybody thinks I'm crazy," Tall Al was known to say. "I'm not crazy; I'm a messenger: Extraterrestrials are here!"

36

Paranormal is at the top of the list.

Long Island is 118 miles long by about 18 miles wide at its widest point. It's a suburb of towering New York City. We have a diverse population of over seven million people crammed into this relatively small area.

Though New York City extends onto Long Island in the form of the heavily populated counties of Queens and Brooklyn, most people regard Nassau and Suffolk Counties as the real "Long Island." Indeed, these two counties eat up the majority of the island's land.

The further east one goes towards the end of the island, out toward the deep mysterious Atlantic Ocean, out towards Montauk, home of the "Montauk Monster," and Camp Hero, where the alleged mind-control experiments of The Montauk Project reportedly took place, the more rural the land becomes.

In Suffolk County, the island's most rural and eastern county, there is a large wine growing region with endless rows of vineyards and dozens of wineries where the grapes are pressed and the wine is bottled. We also have many farms that produce everything from dark green spinach, to yellow corn, to husky "Long Island Spud" potatoes, to orange Halloween pumpkins. People are often surprised to learn Suffolk County leads the state of New York in income derived from the sale of agriculture. Too often people think of Long Island as so heavily populated that it can not support farmlands. But there are many farms in Suffolk County, not so vast in size, but they are productive. In general, it's safe to say there is a very different feeling one gets in suburban Nassau County compared to the more spacious and rural Suffolk County.

So you would be right, dear reader, if you suspected the bulk of Long Island's population is in the western half of the island nearest to New York City. At night, one can see the stars more clearly in the farmlands and in the Pine Barrens of eastern Long Island than in the heavily populated towns and cities in the west, closer to Manhattan. Eastern Long Island is where the Pine Barrens reside in moonlit surrender, and where the UFOs come to hide amid the trees. It's also where agents of the secretive Anti-UFO Army assemble to conduct investigations of the alien visitors to Long Island. It's my belief they are hunting extraterrestrials.

Our island is best known for its fine beaches, wines, spuds, great colleges and universities, fishing, golf courses, the Big Duck, the ritzy Hamptons, fresh seafood, Billy Joel, shipwrecks, good looking girls, and the paranormal. But these days "paranormal" is at the top of the list.

37

Spaceship over the Long Island Sound.

For me, the realization that UFOs were infiltrating Long Island came into focus in 1989 when I was reporting about the haphazard building plans proposed for the Pine Barrens.

This was back when I was harassing builders and politicians with stories about bad building plans and finances that were not adding up. It was at this time that some Long Islanders who pursued UFOs claimed police officers aimed their weapons at a spaceship over dreary Columbia Avenue on the outskirts of pretty Port Jefferson Village.

"Port Jeff," as it's called by people who know it, is a quaint, old harbor village of white buildings that house cute, but expensive, shops, restaurants, bars, and art galleries. The historic village is located on the north shore of mid-Suffolk County. During the daytime, ferries run every hour out of Port Jeff harbor to Bridgeport, Connecticut. The ferries bypass busy New York City and its heavy traffic congestion, carrying people to sweet New England by way of blue water and fresh air.

It was on just such a ferry ride at sunset in early August 2012, while Diane and I were returning home from researching legends of a monster in a lake near the Canadian border in northern Vermont, that we witnessed an enormous, brightly glowing, golden, cigar-shaped object appear out of nowhere in the sky over the darkening waters. The craft floated across the dusky, dark blue heavens over the Long Island Sound near Bridgeport as the mighty ferry thundered towards Port Jeff. Not many people were sitting in the cold wind rushing over the deck at the back of the ship, so we were not surprised that no one else was observing it with us.

We couldn't believe our eyes. The glowing golden object stayed in the sky for a half hour or better before it just slipped into alien obscurity behind red clouds in the western sky and the avalanching sheet of darkness that would eat up the night. I was certain the next day the *New York Times* would have a report about the UFO we saw, but there was nothing in any of the papers. I checked the television news programs the next day, too, but there was nothing mentioned about the appearance of the craft on the television stations either.

My senses were shaken awake when, some months later, I spotted the exact type of brightly-glowing, yellow-orange, cigar-shaped spaceship in a clip about UFOs. The clip was in a documentary related to Dr. Steven Greer's UFO Disclosure Project. In the movie, I found the exact type of craft that Diane and I had seen over the Long Island Sound had also been recorded flying over Stuttgart, Germany in 1997. I recognized the vehicle immediately. No wings, no tail, no smoke, no sound. It moved slowly across the sky over a field in Germany, just like it did over the Long Island Sound south of Bridgeport in August 2012. The huge craft, and others that looked just like it, were revealed in footage of UFOs recorded in different spots around the world in James Fox's no-nonsense and most excellent 2004 documentary, *Out of the Blue*, a movie I would recommend to anybody who wants to hear the truth about UFOs from the mouths of authorities like pilots, generals, astronauts, and presidents.

Diane and I both know what we saw that fateful evening. In fact, it was that unbelievable sighting over the Long Island Sound that led me to make an important decision that would alter our successful careers as *The Paranormal Adventurers*: I decided that week—because of the sighting and because I had for a long time known in my heart of hearts that someday I must write about the UFOs everybody is seeing over Long Island—to take a pause for a few years from ghost investigations on Long Island with Diane to pursue UFOs on my own.

Diane said she understood my intentions and wished me the best. At the time, she said she didn't feel comfortable with the study of UFOs, partly because it was such a big topic to try to understand and prove, and partly because the ridicule Ufologists face is more severe than the ridicule faced by ghost hunters. She learned this early on when she and her girlfriend were playing near their homes in the summer when they were young teenagers and a flying saucer type spacecraft appeared over a neighbor's residential garage, only to hover silently for a brief time, and then disappear. Nobody believed Diane or her friend.

So, I had to excuse myself from our business to do what I needed to do about the UFO problem. It was a big decision for me. For almost a decade Diane and I had been writers and lecturers on the topic of Long Island's ghosts, ghouls, and monsters. Now I was going to leave behind that business that we had lovingly built together. This was the decision that led me to join MUFON and to go out into a graveyard at night with members of a CE-5 group and call alien spaceships down from the heavens.

The study of UFOs was uncharted territory for me at the time because I had never put much effort into researching them. But I had to do it now. Spaceships seemed to be calling me, as they had done years earlier when I was a reporter watching silent machines hovering over the twisted trees in the dark Pine Barrens forest of eastern Long Island; and when I was even younger and I saw a ship on fire in the sky on the day of the 1965 Blackout.

Soon after I made the decision to pursue UFOs, Diane and I took down *The Paranormal Adventurers* website and we refused to take more than a handful of lectures for 2013, so that I would have more time to study the UFO phenomenon.

This was a big departure from the sixty or so speaking engagements we took on in each of the eight years previously. Not lecturing as much as usual would allow me more time to dedicate to researching cases of UFOs, and joining fellow UFO researchers in the field and at MUFON meetings where I could exchange ideas with people who were more knowledgeable on the topic of aliens and spacecrafts than me.

These days, Diane is again joining me in this pursuit of UFOs because she has seen the helicopters over my house and the Men in Black watching her house when I visited her. Lord knows I need her invaluable help with this all-important project.

38

Cops drawing guns on UFOs?

Even today, this back road near Route 25A in Port Jefferson, where cops allegedly pulled out their handguns on a spaceship, is a dismal gray place to venture down. It's dusty and blank, with none of the promise of an exciting, old, lusty, white-painted seaport village just around the corner. The road is near the tired old Long Island Railroad station and, back in 1989, in particular, it cried of loneliness and abandon like roads around railroad stations often do. I wondered, *Why would a spaceship want to come here?*

At this time, I was writing for a newspaper in Medford, located seven miles or so south of Port Jeff. Medford is roughly in the middle of Long Island as one goes north to south across the eighteen miles of the island's width. I had a desk in the strip mall office. The storefront was located on Route 112 in Medford, the same road, and in the same town, from which Janet Russell claims she was abducted, brought into a spaceship, and told by Grays that aliens are breeding with humans.

The Medford storefront where the newspaper was located was one of many satellite offices the tabloid owned. We had offices all over Long Island. Our headquarters was in Farmingdale.

My gray desk was big and old with a portable beige Macintosh computer sitting on top. This was back when Macs used 1.44 megabyte diskettes. I'd bring my computer home with me at night sometimes. It wasn't exactly a laptop. The monitor and the disk drive were in the same portable unit. It was big, bulky, and slow as malaises.

My desk at the office was situated beside the immense storefront window with vertical blinds that kept out the hot sun. I'd put my feet up on the desk and turn to my left and dream as I gazed out the window through the slits of the blinds. It was the best spot in the office. There were no other windows in the office because other stores were attached to the right and left sides of our storefront. The store wasn't wide, but it was deep like a railroad car.

Deeper in the room were five or six other gray desks with other reporters tapping away at their portable beige Macintosh computers. A few editors worked on their Macs in an airless room at the other end of the newsroom. The editors didn't have any windows to gaze out. Farther back in the store, in other unseen rooms of mystery cut off from us, were cubicles belonging to salespeople and sales managers who had desks and telephones. Their phones rang all the time. They often had pizza parties and made a lot of noise. They went home at 5 p.m.

Outside my window I could see everything that took place in the blacktop parking lot. Across a few rows of parking stalls marked by yellow lines were a series of stores facing my office. They mirrored exactly the row of storefronts in which the newspaper was situated. The same property owner managed the two rows of one-story stores and the small parking lot in-between the two strip malls.

Sometimes beautiful women left the cleaners or some other small store across the way and I watched them get into their cars through the slits of the blinds. Other times big men smoking cigarettes spit out their car windows as they grumpily waited for their tired wives to get off work from one of the stores. I was usually alone in the office after five and was thus the only one to witness all this. The parking lot outside my window was empty after the wives went home. Mostly, the reporters and editors I worked with treated their workday as nine-to-five jobs. I was no nine-to-fiver. That's why I had the desk near the window. (All this information will be of value to you when I discuss the men in federal cars who watched me when I started writing stories related to UFOs – so bare with me; we will get there, dear reader.)

When I was at the office working, pursuing the police beat or town political scene, mostly on the phone, I usually ended up rushing out with my gray overcoat trailing behind me and my portable police scanner in hand to cover a murder, robbery, or some kind of meeting.

I knew dreary Columbia Avenue in Port Jefferson well. I knew the very spot where supposed witnesses saw cops allegedly take aim, and may have even shot at a UFO that reportedly came down out of the sky for some strange reason and shook a U.S. Mail truck with the driver in it.

So, one evening when I was alone in the office, I called a friend of mine with the Suffolk County Police Department, who I often relied upon for background information. He was straight with me. He insisted officers would never pull their weapons on a spacecraft because federal law makes it illegal to shoot at an airplane or any other kind of vehicle in the sky. He said this was basic stuff in which cops are trained—but that he'd ask around about the incident anyhow.

"Maybe one of the street dicks knows something about it, because I don't," he said.

But, two days later, he called me back and reported he came up with nothing. In the meantime, I checked the police blotter at the Sixth Precinct in Coram. The blotter is a book with summaries of the complaints police responded to in the precinct during the week. I found nothing about a UFO appearing in Port Jefferson on the night in question.

I walked around the bleak area of the uninteresting road in Port Jeff where members of LIUFON insisted cops were prepared to fire upon—or did fire upon—an alien space machine. I found nothing. No bullet casings, no ground markings, no yellow police tape, no burnt grass. I discovered nothing that would reveal a spaceship had visited the area or that cops were at this spot, possibly shooting their pistols at a craft only days before.

I wrote a story for the newspaper that said according to police there were no UFOs over Port Jefferson on the night cops allegedly shot at—or at least took aim at—a spaceship, that the story was false, that UFO enthusiasts must have made it up. I presented the UFO side of the story, too. I told the public that UFO enthusiasts were saying cops were covering up the spaceship incident. The cops did this routinely, they said, as part of the tapestry of conspiracy that every level of government has been weaving since the 1947 Roswell, New Mexico, spaceship crash to hide the fact that UFOs are here and that aliens are in our skies watching us. I said it all in a matter-of-fact reporter way with very little personality, so that it didn't seem that I took sides. In my mind, however, I was siding with the cops on this one. These UFO people were crazy!

Ultimately, I was surprised to find as the days passed that nobody seemed to care about the UFO story I wrote, one way or another. I didn't receive any mail or calls about the article. I remember wondering why nobody cared. I knew we had a large readership. Readers wrote and called me freely with comments about every other story, it seemed. I wondered why readers weren't reacting to this inflammatory discussion.

In the years after this time I learned that people are almost mechanically tuned out of discussions about UFOs and the notion that spaceships are in our skies. They switch off, ignoring everything, as though they had been instructed to disregard such important information and then to forget that they were instructed to tune UFOs out. I remember reading in a book that a UFO was spotted above a busy intersection in Manhattan in broad daylight, but almost nobody cared, even though the UFO was pointed out to them and they could clearly see it. The apathy on Long Island is profound. How can you fight an enemy when nobody cares?

39

The Moriches Bay UFO shoot-down.

Moriches Bay as seen from a dock in Center Moriches.

Then the UFO people of LIUFON made another, more alarming claim, also in 1989.

They said a spaceship was shot down into the cold black waters of Moriches Bay at night by U.S. military jets that left seventeen aliens dead and a wrecked spaceship steaming in the water. The bodies of the aliens, they said, were collected from the wreckage by government operatives from the Anti-UFO Army, black-ops stuff, and nobody was allowed anywhere in the area while all this was going on. Allegedly, the incident disrupted the hamlet of Center Moriches for two days. Supposedly, people in the area were not allowed to leave their homes if they lived south of Montauk Highway, a narrow road a mile or so north of the bay. They were misinformed about the reasons. This amounted to a large area about a mile long by a mile wide, where people were reportedly forced to stay on their own properties while the aliens and their craft were fetched out of the bay. Yet not a word about this was said on television, the radio, in newspapers, or spoken about at the local barber shop or in the churches. How could this be?

Years later, I would hear the story about that day from Carmela Somma. She lived in Manorville, the hamlet located just north of Center Moriches, nearest to the Long Island Expressway in the middle of Long Island.

Old Carmela leaned over the cherry wood table in her sunny dining room with a cup of coffee aimed at my chin, telling her story, making another point, splashing the coffee without blinking her eyes, leaning her whole body towards me, insisting it was all true. This was before she died at age 80, just months after we talked.

Mrs. Somma said the day of the spaceship downing in Moriches Bay was also the very day a Canadian goose fell dead out of the sky with a loud thump in her long dirt driveway. Her driveway led into her three acres of "horse property " in the Pine Barrens woods. Her house was built before anyone knew how valuable the Pine Barrens were to Long Island. She said this Canadian goose incident occurred the same day a large black crow flew right into the thick bay window of her living room. The bird broke its neck as it went through the glass pane. It lay dead on her living room floor. She just stood above it, staring breathlessly in confusion. She showed me the very spot on the floor where the crow lay dead in a pool of its own blood. She narrated the story, trying to get me to see the bird in my mind's eye. I did.

Carmela remembered the peculiar, eerie way the dust rose like a mushroom from the dry dirt driveway when the goose hit the ground at terminal velocity, about 125 miles an hour, "because it fell from high up," she insisted. She said military types in uniforms and sunglasses with crew cuts and big knuckle rings were all over the area that day. They pulled over in front of her house as she was burying the goose and the crow near a special large pine tree, like a Christmas tree, that her father planted in her front yard when she was a young woman and she and her husband just moved into their newly built home in the woods. At the time of the goose's death, Carmela's house was one of only a few houses in the area. The rest of the island thereabouts featured big potato and squash farms. The road that passed in front of her house led to the bay located at least five miles south.

The government men asked Mrs. Somma questions about where they could buy coffee and gas, and the best way to get to the bay.

"Moriches Bay is down south," she told them with one closed eye to the late afternoon sunlight. "Just keep driving," she advised.

Carmela looked in the open car windows at the Army-like brief cases and shiny police-like badges and knew something big and official was going on in the area on this strangest of days. She sensed it was about some kind of trouble in the skies. After all, on this day she buried a dead goose that fell out of the sky and a crow that busted through the bay window in her living room. She knew something was wrong in Long Island's skies.

How, though, could she have known it was an alien spaceship, possibly emitting poisonous gas or anti-orgone energy?

97

40

TWA Flight 800 explosion over Moriches Bay.

ABOVE: Quietly situated behind a wall of landscaping at Smith Point Beach on Fire Island in Shirley is a memorial for the 230 victims of TWA Flight 800 Explosion.
BELOW: A man looks out at the Atlantic Ocean. It was ten miles out over Moriches Bay where Flight 800 exploded and rained down to the water, as beachgoers and campers at Smith Point County Park watched in horror.

Moriches Bay is the same body of water where TWA Flight 800 went down seventeen years after the alleged Moriches Bay shoot-down. All 230 passengers and crew aboard the Boeing jumbo jet were killed when it exploded on July 17, 1996, twelve minutes into its flight out of JKF International Airport, located on Long Island.

After an exhaustive investigation, the federal government determined the cause of the TWA Flight 800 explosion was a spark that ignited fuel fumes in the jet's center fuel tank. But some people who witnessed the terrible explosion said they saw "something" approaching the jet before it exploded. Naneen Levine, for one, told ABC News she saw a "red dot" go up towards the jet just before it exploded. The sudden explosion immediately sheered off a third of the plane. Some of the eye

witnesses said they believed what they saw might have been a missile. Janet Russell, the psychic (see section 34), said she was present at Smith Point Beach that day and saw the explosion. She said she knew the plane was going to explode long before it did; she predicted it, she said. "It was a missile," she told me. "I believe I'm psychic today because I was abducted," she explained.

ABOVE: The TWA Flight 800 International Memorial.
BELOW: The names of all 230 passengers and crew who died in the explosion on July 17, 1996 are written into a granite wall.

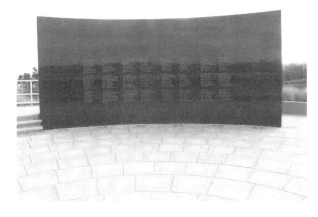

Pierre Salinger, a former ABC News correspondent and white house Press Secretary under Presidents John F. Kennedy and Lyndon B. Johnson, spearheaded claims that friendly fire from a U.S. Navy ship brought down the 747. He claimed a missile was launched from the USS *Normandy* by mistake, striking the jet on its way to Paris, France, and the friendly fire was then covered up by the government. This claim was repeatedly denied by the Feds.

The FBI had 1,000 agents assigned to the case at the time. Government agents were frantic to present then-President Bill Clinton with a plausible cause for the explosion because terrorism was suspected, specifically terrorists out of Iran, and he had to have information quickly to react accordingly. But evidence supporting such a hypothesis, such as characteristic signature pock marks in metal caused by explosives of a bomb or a missile, were never found on the plane's parts retrieved from the ocean. It quickly became apparent to investigators that terrorism was not a factor, the government reported at the time.

In the spring of 2013, however, came an announcement that contradicts the government's claims of a spark causing the explosion. Six former federal investigators claimed TWA Flight 800 was shot out of the sky by a missile, and their beliefs were in a new documentary. Supposedly, these investigators waited seventeen years to make the announcement because they feared their federal retirement pensions could have been in jeopardy if they spoke out against the government's official findings in 2000.

The Federal Aviation Administration's (FAA) final report in 2000 about the incident said there was no missile involved. The report said a central fuel tank exploded—end of story. The explosion cut the first third of the plane, including the first-class passenger section and the cockpit, away from the rest of the jet and that section fell into the ocean. For thirty seconds, the remaining two thirds of the aircraft continued to soar through the sky before it, too, tumbled and exploded, raining down in "a million pieces" into the bay.

Many people believed that a missile from a man-made object brought the 747 down. Then again, maybe it had something to do with UFOs, some people suggested.

In 2013, the government reiterated its 2000 findings, saying the evidence six retired investigators brought forth in the documentary was inaccurate. Nonetheless, the six investigators began a petition calling for the National Transportation Safety Board to reopen the investigation.

According to a Foxnews.com story published on June 19, 2013, Jim Speer, who was "an accident investigator for the Airline Pilots Association and one of a half-dozen experts seeking a new review of the probe, said, 'We don't know who fired the missile, but we have a lot more confidence that it was a missile.'"

Foxnews.com also quoted Tom Stalcup, "a physicist who is considered one of the foremost independent researchers, and participated in the documentary," saying at a press conference, "It all fits like a glove. It is what it is and all the evidence is there."

According to the six experts who are challenging the government to review the case, investigators from the NTSB were not allowed to investigate the explosion once the FBI took over the investigation. The plane had been reassembled in a hangar for study. "It's obvious that the truth was not allowed to be pursued," said Jim Speer in the Foxnews.com story. "A majority of people working in that hangar did not feel as if the evidence was properly being handled," he added.

41

UFOs and USOs.

Since the TWA Flight 800 explosion, a lot of speculation has surfaced about extraterrestrials hiding under the surface of Moriches Bay in Unidentified Submergible Objects (USOs). Since then, too, UFOs were spotted by pilots over this bay and researchers have shown that these incidents were well documented.

According to Preston Dennett, author of *UFOs Over New York: A True History of Extraterrestrial Encounters in the Empire State*, the captain and crew of a 747 Jumbo from Saudi Arabia reported seeing a "green, flare-like" object over their jet when they were in the exact area where Flight 800 exploded and went into the ocean five months earlier. Though the plane was headed to JFK, it was diverted to Dulles Airport in Washington, D.C.

Dennett wrote:

> Interestingly, the day after this new UFO report surfaced in the media, CNN was told by the FBI that the report "could be explained by a meteor shower." The brief segment explaining the sighting was aired over and over again on the news.
>
> However, what most news reports didn't say is that the Saudi crew not only sighted the green, flare-like object, but it actually appeared on their onboard radar. Let's see ...a glowing green object that "hung over" the plane and appeared on radar; obviously, this was no meteor.

According to Dennett, the crew of another plane spotted a UFO in the same area of Moriches Bay where the Flight 800 explosion took place only a month before the Saudi Arabian crew had their encounter. Dennett wrote that the story of the sighting was "effectively suppressed until the Saudi Arabian Jumbo Jet UFO encounter was leaked to the press."

Dennett claimed, in November 1996, the captain and crew of yet a third airliner saw a UFO over Moriches Bay in the same spot where Flight 800 went down. The captain of a Swissair 747, on the way to JFK, reported to air traffic control in Boston, Massachusetts, a near miss with a white object traveling the opposite direction and flying right over the airplane. The author of *UFOs Over New York* was kind enough to include a transcript of the actual conversation between the Swissair pilot and the air traffic controller:

SWISSAIR: Sir, I don't know what it was, but it just flew like a couple of hundred feet above us. I don't know if it was a rocket, or whatever, but incredibly fast in the opposite direction.
    CONTROLLER: In the opposite direction?
    SWISSAIR: Yes sir, it was too fast to be an airplane.

Dennett writes:

> The FBI's official explanation of the TWA streak of light and the Saudi Arabian and Pakistani jet UFO sightings is meteors: they made no announcement of the Swissair sighting. However, obviously now credulity has been stretched to the limit.

42

Reports of mutilated animals.
Back to 1989.

Admittedly, if the UFO people hadn't gotten my attention yet with a story about cops shooting at a spaceship in Port Jefferson, or the downing of an alien vehicle over Moriches Bay, they were about to.

It was when they talked about animal mutilations that my vision of what was going on with UFOs over Long Island became clearer. I was working on a few stories about animal mutilations on my own at the time, separate from any notion of aliens from out of space committing the horrid acts.

One story I had written for the paper, for example, was about a farmer in the Ridge-Calverton area who told me he came to work in the morning and found goats, sheep, rabbits, and chickens dead. These animals were on display for children to appreciate. But now they were dead. And not just dead, mutilated. And not just mutilated, but surgically dissected. The animals' organs were cleanly and precisely removed. It seemed sex organs were the type mostly missing.

Whoever cut out the animal innards took the organs with them off the property: "What kind of sick minds would do this?" asked the stunned farmer.

Initially, I suspected the animal killers were misguided kids who might have been drunk and out to prove themselves tough by skinning helpless animals in surgical ways with ultra sharp knives. But when I really got to thinking about it, the possibility of drunk and disorderly kids surgically removing animal organs at night in the middle of a farm without leaving any traces of blood—while they were drunk—seemed doubtful.

This was the same kind of atrocity members of LIUFON, headed by founder John Ford, had been talking about when they came to see me and hand me drawings of extraterrestrials and spaceships. This was seven years before Ford was arrested and imprisoned.

Ford came into the newspaper office often to talk to me, and anybody else who would listen to him speak, on the subject of UFOs over Long Island, about which he was clearly an expert. The reporters rolled their eyes and told him to go tell the editors what he had to say because they were too busy getting their weekly load of stories done. The truth is they were just plain not interested in what he had to say.

But I talked to Ford.

He was a kindly person with sad, brown engaging eyes.

He showed me drawings and sketches of Grays and Nordics and told me stories about abductions and UFOs in the skies over Long Island. Then he invited me to a UFO conference to be held at the Community Center at the Artist Lake Condominium Complex in Middle Island in April of 1989. It was to be an all-day event and was very expensive. Later, after he left, I spoke to the editor, who called our managing editor in Farmingdale who said the newspaper would pick up the cost if I wanted to attend the conference. I called John Ford and the deal was set. As it would turn out, I would be the only reporter present.

There might have been a few hundred people at the Artist Lake UFO Conference. Many were noted UFO researchers. Budd Hopkins, the famous UFO abductions researcher, was one of them. I interviewed him at length. I saw in his eyes there was more to spaceships than I knew. It was time for me to wake up.

A woman spoke. She said spaceships floated over her house and even landed in her backyard. She said she lived in the Pine Barrens of Manorville. She felt like the aliens now controlled her, that they were in her head. I can now relate to this, though I wouldn't describe myself as "controlled" by them. I would say, however, that they are in my head.

43

Dead bullfrogs at Southaven Park.

I was in my office mulling over police blotter items related to the appearance of The Lady in White, a ghost often seen in the wee hours of the night outside

Union Cemetery on Route 25 in Middle Island, when I received a telephone call from a nervous woman who lived near Southaven Park in Shirley. She said she had taken a walk to the pond in the park and found dozens of dead bullfrogs. The body of water she referred to was actually a part of the Carman's River. She wanted to know if I'd be interested in taking a look at the dead frogs and if I'd be willing to investigate the matter to determine the cause of their deaths.

"Of course," I said, and I arranged to meet her the next day and see what she found.

Sure enough, bloated, pale-green bullfrogs floated dead at the banks of the pond in Southaven Park. They had been deceased for days. There were perhaps two dozen carcasses.

The next day, I got hold of a scientist at the Department of Environmental Conservation (DEC) who was the person to speak to in such matters and I relayed the information. The investigator and I knew each other well from the many articles I had written that he contributed to by helping me with scientific information or with comments that were of value.

He said, "Dead bullfrogs, huh? That's strange. Something's wrong there. I mean, well, heck, we have to pay attention to incidents like these because the respiratory system of a frog is very similar to a human's. If a frog is sick, we could get sick. Often it's pollution or viruses that cause the death of frogs. I'll look into the matter and get back to you."

Now, this is where the story turns suddenly strange: he never called me back.

Days went by before I finally called the scientist again to find out what caused the deaths of the bullfrogs. It was queer that he hadn't gotten back to me because he always responded in a punctual way. He knew I was up against a deadline.

Then the scientist would not take my calls. I had to hold the story for the next week. His secretary told me he was busy all day. This happened for a few days in a row. Finally, when by chance I reached him at home (which pissed him off big-time because it breaks an unwritten rule of privacy), he seemed to want to get off the telephone right away, as if the phone was tapped, as if someone was listening in. Rather than tell me what autopsies of the bullfrogs revealed, he merely speculated about a virus that the bullfrogs might have caught from pet frogs that someone might have released into the same pond where the bullfrogs were found dead.

"It was probably a virus," said the nervous scientist.

"Probably?" I asked. "Shouldn't you know for sure? Didn't you say frogs have a respiratory system very much like a human's respiratory system and that what affects bullfrogs could affect us?"

The scientist seemed to want to get off the phone right away. This was very strange behavior for him.

"You did perform autopsies on these animals, right? You did take samples for toxicological study, right?

"Yes, we have them," the scientist said. "But I have to go."

He seemed terribly nervous and agitated that I kept him on the phone. What could have been so pressing that this usually passive, relaxed man should turn so nervous?

"But wait," I said. "What about...."

And the telephone clicked. He'd hung up.

"I called him back a dozen times in the next few days, but he wouldn't take my calls.

It was at this time I started to notice sets of two men at a time—men with crew cuts in suits—sitting in official government-cop-looking cars in the parking lot across from my office after hours. Unlike most cars, these were always backed-in against the stores across the way so that the driver and passenger faced the newspaper office in which I was the sole occupant. All the wives had already been picked up from the stores by their husbands, all the shops were closed. I was the only person remaining in any of the stores in the strip mall. All the newspaper people were gone. The men watched the office without talking. I studied them through the slits of the vertical blinds. They looked official. They looked like cops.

In one case, when it was time to go, I gathered my things and suddenly noticed through the slits that the car was gone. I quickly left the building and hurriedly drove out of the lot. But as I drove onto Route 112 in the direction of home, I spotted the car with the two federal-looking agents in suits behind me. *What the hell?* I wondered. I drove for some time, switching lanes and even roads. The car stayed right behind me, the hard-looking agents inside letting me know they were there.

I didn't know if it was my imagination or if men were really following me. *Why would anybody want to follow me?* I wondered. I thought of all the builders who I might have angered with my articles about how their proposed construction projects could contribute to the ruination of the Pine Barrens. They stood to lose a lot of money if their projects fell through. Maybe one of the builders had enough of my contradictory articles. Maybe one of them was going to punish me, grab me, murder me, and bury me in the same woods I was trying to protect.

Eventually, the government car turned off. I took a deep breath.

The same kind of thing happened several times over the next two weeks. I started to grow paranoid. My telephone clicked sometimes while I was talking. I took the telephone on my desk apart to see if it was tapped with a bugging device. I looked under the desk and around on the walls to see if a bug had been planted in the office. *What would they want with me?* I wondered.

These incidents occurred during the same weeks I was repeatedly calling back the doctor scientist at the DEC who was handling the case of the dead bullfrogs. At last, when I caught him off guard and he unwittingly answered his phone, he told me he didn't know what killed them, that I should just tell readers it was probably a virus. "I can't help you with this any more, do you understand?" he asked.

I realized then that he was under duress. He was probably being watched just like me. His phone was probably being tapped just like mine.

Why?

My editor was disappointed once again that the space he reserved for the article I planned to write about the results of studies of the dead bullfrogs could not be filled. He asked me to attach just a few paragraphs to the local police blotter in which I reported some of the calls police responded to in the local neighborhoods. Then I was to be finished with the bullfrogs story forever. I'd wash my hands of it and concentrate on more substantial stories.

The editor said, "You should just do what the scientist guy said, and just tell our readers it was a virus that killed the bullfrogs. I mean, who are you to say he's wrong? He's a doctor with the DEC, for Pete sake!"

He was right, so that's what I did. But it didn't feel right. Something was going on that I couldn't decipher.

44

The 1992 Southaven Park spaceship crash.

Inside Southaven County Park in Shirley. This is the site where an alleged spaceship crashed in 1992.

The darkest place on Long Island, a place of legends and mystery, occupies thousands of acres of suspicious land and waterway in the Pine Barrens of the south shore of eastern Long Island. If one should fly over this place at night, as federal agents in dark helicopters often do, for their own secretive reasons, one would suddenly leave the lights of local hamlets behind and be swallowed up into the darkness of the ancient Pine Barrens of Long Island. The crawling tidal swamps of the Carmans River carry ancient secrets away to the Great South Bay and then into the ocean.

In 1992, a small silvery spaceship supposedly crashed near this swampy river in these old woods, close to where the bullfrogs were found dead a few years earlier.

There are those people who claim that the craft that crashed at the park was accompanied by another craft. The stories I heard blamed one craft for crashing into the other due to pilot error. Both ended up going down.

What follows is based on what I read and heard on the street: The second spaceship went down into the woods belonging to Brookhaven National Lab., five miles away, where it exploded. It's alleged. There is no proof of this second spaceship. In fact, there is questionable proof of the crashing of the first spaceship. Members of LIUFON said, at the time, the public never had access to the truth about the crashes, so how could we ever know what really happened?

Some people believe to this day the bodies of extraterrestrials were recovered from the downed alien vehicle in Southaven Park by soldiers belonging to a secretive Anti-UFO Army that works outside of even the president's, the CIA's, and the FBI's control.

45

Extraterrestrials on ice?

According to UFO conspiracy theorists, the alien bodies that were retrieved at Southaven Park were taken to and autopsied at Brookhaven National Laboratory, a heavily guarded U.S. Department of Energy facility, located five miles north in the woods of a place called Upton. It has been suggested the corpses of the dead aliens are today stored at the top-secret government facility, or perhaps even Area 51 in Nevada, a place where deadly force to stop unwanted visitors is the U.S. Government's official policy for keeping its privacy. Or the bodies might be in freezers in Florida, where comedian Jackie Gleason reportedly once went to view the bodies as a fun lark with President Richard Nixon while he was in office, to view dead space aliens for entertainment. Gleason couldn't eat or sleep for days after seeing the dead extraterrestrials, it's been reported. The President and Gleason were good friends. President Nixon even picked Gleason

The sign announcing "the Lab."

The entrance to Brookhaven National Laboratory in Upton. Were bodies of dead aliens brought here after the 1992 Southaven County Park spaceship crash, as some people claimed at the time?

up in a regular car that he was driving without Secret Service agents in entourage. This was the night they went to see the stored extraterrestrials.

46

Spaceship crash cover-up?

Long Island conspiracy theorists are apt to say the alleged spaceship crash at Southaven Park discussed prior was immediately covered up by the government so that people wouldn't know the reality of extraterrestrials visiting Earth. They rarely point out that it is likely the Anti-UFO Army is suppressing information because they are trying to protect us from panic. The leaders of the Anti-UFO Army seem to know the aliens visiting us are using us in experiments, and they are doing the best to understand the nature of these beings so they can defeat them. Or...so we have to assume. The Anti-UFO Army is trying to fight back on our behalf. So we hope. We have to support them, and if we can, contribute by following their orders, as long as they are sensible and profitable in the war against the alien invasion. We who know firsthand must share our experiences involving extraterrestrials with the Anti-UFO Army and with the public, so we can figure out where they congregate and why, and to better understand how we as a species are evolving with these beings. They have been on Long Island in an obvious way now for about sixty years, according to various calculations. But it's likely they have been with Mankind for millennia.

47

Spaceship on fire crashes into parkland.

Allegedly, people claimed to have seen a spaceship breaking apart in mid-air over busy State Route 27, also known as Sunrise Highway, at about seven o'clock in the evening on November 24, 1992. Pieces of the fiery craft were said to have slammed into the woods in the nearby Suffolk County's Southaven Park, 1,356 acres of Pine Barrens and river.

According to alleged eye witness reports, the small, silver craft tumbled awkwardly out of the sky, like an egg lobbed through the air, before it exploded into red and yellow flames and rained down in fiery fragments into the trees.

LIUFON investigators, headed by John Ford, quickly took up the challenge of pursuing leads into the matter. A newspaper report of the incident, inspired by LIUFON, appeared six months later in the local *South Shore Press*. It quoted anonymous people who were at the scene as saying they saw state and local police officers directing traffic away from the park. Insignias for the governmental agencies for which some of the officers worked—closest to the wreckage—were absent from their black uniforms.

The park was closed for four days following the alleged incident. Coincidentally, this was the same park where I reported bullfrogs dying mysteriously in large numbers in a pond three years before the alleged spaceship crash.

People who lived immediately outside the park reported power brownouts and blackouts occurring at the time of the alleged UFO impact. One such person told her story years later to investigators of the History Channel's television show *UFO Hunters* when researchers, headed up by Bill Birnes, investigated the Southaven Park incident for a two-part series. Though investigators for the show were thorough, in the end, the evidence they gathered was inconclusive as to whether or not a spaceship actually crashed in Southaven Park seventeen years earlier.

One fact that clearly emerged from the *UFO Hunters* investigation was that on the night of the supposed incident, the Brookhaven Fire Department had been called to the scene, but firefighters were quickly told to turn back to the firehouse because they were informed that firemen from the federally controlled Brookhaven National Laboratory in Upton would handle the fire. The laboratory's 848 acres of property is located north of the park in the Pine Barrens. It's all woods in between.

On the night of the incident, an anonymous firefighter with a video camera recorded pieces of an object he believed to be debris from the spacecraft being handled by authorities at the scene. He claimed to have recorded dead alien bodies on the ground in the area of the crash. His film, which was given to the Long Island UFO Network anonymously, can be found by searching "UFO Crash on Long Island NY from 1992 Part 1." (Here's the link: http://www.youtube.com/watch?v=LgtFrfrvcWk.) The search should take you to a *UFO Hunters* show that deals with the video. Viewers to the above website will also find excellent analysis of the video by the expert *UFO Hunters* investigators. Many viewers of the 1992 recording complain they are left frustrated by the movie's poor quality. The nighttime recording is murky and objects are indistinct.

Members of LIUFON said that at the time of the supposed Southaven Park crash, bodies of dead space aliens were transported from the crash site to Brookhaven National Laboratory. UFO enthusiasts have long speculated the spaceship crashed in the area of the lab while its alien occupants were spying on experiments being conducted there. Such experiments at the lab at the time reportedly included military experiments. Many local residents suspect scientists of conducting secret experiments at the site—a suspicion lab spokespeople say is ridiculous.

Is it?

The government, meanwhile, has always maintained Southaven Park caught fire by human means and that a UFO never crashed there. Park officials claimed the park was closed following the fire to accommodate duck hunters, not to keep out eyewitnesses who might see the military removing classified debris.

The May 25, 1993 *South Shore Press* article quoted John Ford:

> "We found an area that was burned out and some trees were bent over," Ford recalled. "A section looked like it had been plowed over by machinery."
>
> But two things were of particular interest to Ford: "We were getting a higher than normal radiation reading in the area, higher than regular background radiation, and the fence line in that area," said Ford, "had no magnetic reading."
>
> Ford explained that metal fences maintain a magnetic charge from the Earth. "Something had stripped away the magnetic charge of the fence," he said.

The *South Shore Press* also discussed the aforementioned video produced by the anonymous firefighter who was said to be at the crash site on the night of the supposed fire. Members of LIUFON insisted the video showed spaceship debris and dead aliens:

The video, a copy of which was given to *South Shore Press*, shows people examining a bright reddish, metallic-type object about four-square feet that appears to be emitting a white, cloudy gas, and a hissing sound can be heard—a sight and sound that resembles dry ice that has been exposed to warmer temperatures.

The next shot shows what appears to be a person trying to lift up a body near a tree, but the poor quality of the film makes positive identification impossible. In a final scene, three uniformed men (wearing dark jackets and rounded caps similar to federal swat teams) are seen placing a large shiny spread (similar to Mylar) over something on the ground.

Seated in the canteen at the prison hospital where he is doing time, Ford told Diane and me that boxes of video tapes and photos, and many files containing upwards of a thousand interviews of people who experienced UFOs on Long Island, were stolen from a storage office in years following his arrest. He suspects the boxes were stolen by police. When I suggested the tapes and files might have been stolen by the Anti-UFO Army, he blinked at me and nodded.

"There's one thing that you should tell your readers," said Ford. "I know for sure that all police officers are issued a handbook that they have to follow that instructs them what to do in the event they encounter a person who reports a UFO. The handbook tells them to not report it, and if they see anything to deny it. Tell your readers this because this is how information about UFOs is suppressed from the outset. It's the first layer of denial."

"I will," I said. Since then I have spoken to a few cops who—as Ford would suggest—denied this claim.

PART IV

CHAPTER EIGHT

THE CONTINUOUS SEARCH FOR ANSWERS

48

They respond.

You must remember, though I am a ghost hunter and writer of books about Long Island's subterranean paranormal world, by now UFOs, extraterrestrials, Men in Black, and the secretive Anti-UFO Army agents were the focus of my daily attentions—not ghosts.

So, by the time I went out searching for the Long Island Devil with my old ghost hunting friends Ralph and Dennis, I had virtually run out of interest in anything other than aliens and their interruptions of my life. I had become obsessed with their weird, incomprehensible communications, the strange coincidences and connections I was discovering to everything everywhere. But mostly what I wanted to know is what did they want with me? I was floored by the fact that an extraterrestrial life form with an intelligence far beyond any human's, and from an advanced civilization probably from a far-off planet, actually wanted to communicate with me merely because I tried contacting them through a CE-5 meditation at night in a graveyard in Yaphank.

It seemed too simple. Their response and almost immediate presence seemed all too accessible.

Then it dawned on me that maybe that's the alien's secret weapon: they respond. When I got thinking about it, I realized I had never asked aliens to show themselves to me, though I have done such with ghosts and actually seen a few and experienced many paranormal events as a result. It kind of made some sense to me that they would appear in my life if I asked them to appear.

Could making a connection with an alien civilization really be as easy as meditating and inviting them to Earth? An hour of mediation in a graveyard at night and the deal is done? A few mental pictures sent out into space and contact is made? Were the other members of the CE-5 group experiencing this? When I spoke up early-on with a comment on the group's Internet posting board, I was effectively shut down. All I got back were a few comments from fellow members that said maybe I didn't really see what I thought I saw; that maybe I saw something else that makes more logical sense, like an airplane. When I asked a few members had they been experiencing anything odd in their lives, they said they had not.

The question concerning me now was: Do aliens become permanent fixtures in one's life after contact is made? Do the space visitors believe that because a person contacts them, they are entitled to experiment on that person, to visit him or her while sleeping, to insert sub-miniature microchips into that person's shoulder, even cause unexplainable rashes on the subject's wrists and forearms, and general confusion in that person's mental states? Do they manipulate a person's mind without him or her even realizing it? Were they trying to improve humans or use them? Were they trying to give me insights and knowledge, or destroy me by killing my credibility, showing me things nobody would believe so that whatever I say I saw and experienced would be discredited and discarded?

This brings us back to the Long Island Devil. I felt the Devil was somehow a piece of the enormous puzzle to understanding what was going on with aliens on Long Island.

Call it a hunch or a gut feeling, but I felt if I could only track down the Long Island Devil, photograph it, record it on video, communicate with it and find out what planet it came from and what it wants, then maybe I could uncover a mystery that has been experienced since ancient times that would help me make sense out of my new connection to Earth's space visitors. Moreover, if I could gain an understanding of this creature, perhaps I could contribute to the knowledge base about space creatures, and that would help everyone. In other words, if the elusive Long Island Devil was an extraterrestrial of the clan of extraterrestrials that seem to rule the sky, the Grays and Insectoids, then I might be able to record their stories and tell the world what is going on with them.

Far as I know, I am the only person still attempting to track the Long Island Devil with any commitment. While I don't have an answer as to why I'm the only person still interested in exposing the Long Island Devil to the world, I can tell you I do it because I feel I have a responsibility to find it.

I never did believe the Long Island Devil was a ghost. It had a physical side to it that was more extraterrestrial than spirit. In that way, it was much like Bigfoot. Bigfoot are known to appear when UFOs are seen in the skies, but they are physical, not spiritual—even if they are known to teleport and disappear, just like the Long Island Devil.

"But how is the Devil connected to aliens?" I'd ask myself while looking in the mirror in the morning, feeling the hunch in my gut and a renewed eagerness to explore this mystery.

I'd go to bed wondering, *What has the Long Island Devil to do with extraterrestrials? Is it one?* These questions would poke at my brain all night long.

I'd sit alone at a picnic table in Southaven Park in Shirley and ask myself:

Did the Long Island Devil survive a spaceship crash here in 1992 and then hide in the woods to survive being hunted by soldiers in black uniforms from the Anti-UFO Army who continually chase after it?

Or is the Devil an extraterrestrial that survived a gun battle with military helicopters over Moriches Bay in 1989 and was able to escape capture?

Has an extraterrestrial been dodging soldiers from the Anti-UFO Army for a quarter of a century? Is that possible?

Was the Devil an extraterrestrial left behind by its spaceship crew because the spaceship was shot out of the sky over Moriches Bay in 1989 by military helicopters while a lone extraterrestrial was on the ground a mile away doing field research?

Had the rest of the crew been killed? Does the single alien now walk alone at night in the woods?

Is that why thunderous military helicopters fly over the Pine Barrens with their sinister spotlights aimed down like missiles at the trees?

Are Anti-UFO agents searching for the alien in the wrong area of Long Island?

How long can an extraterrestrial live on its own on our planet?

How did it get to Farmingdale from eastern Long Island without being spotted?

These are the questions I was asking myself daily.

*

One evening, at the end of April 2013, while alone cleaning my home office, it dawned on me that what I really wanted to do was not just settle for having a few experiences with aliens, the meaning of which I didn't understand because their purpose in making contact with me was impossible to grasp; but to take the results of the first CE-5 meeting a huge step further, and make direct contact with our planet's visitors face-to-face. I would have to pursue CE-5 with vigor and find out what the space beings wanted with me. But I'd have to do it secretly, so I wouldn't be thought a lunatic by others, including the people I meditated with in the graveyard that initial cold, dark night. I would ask the aliens why they were they on planet Earth. And specifically, why Long Island? Lastly, why were they showing me things that I couldn't understand? What was the point?

I didn't think anyone would believe anything I had to say regarding my paranormal experiences with spaceships and the clumsy beings I have come to think of as Men in Black, who seemed to show up at the oddest places. These would include the shaven-headed man bumping into strangers on a lonely street in woebegone Lakeview, and the skinny, toothy, balding, sneering little man with glasses taking pictures of Diane's house like a lurid pervert—the house where I was staying at the time, incidentally. And this would also include the grotesque brown globular image lingering at the edge of my yard watching my house only to disappear. Remember the federal agents in the cars watching me after everyone else left the newsroom? What of them? Why was I being followed even back in 1989?

I couldn't blame anyone for doubting my stories about seeing gigantic airplanes hanging like toys on strings in the midnight sky—and the daytime skies as well. It all sounds too preposterous, insane even, I know.

49

Second appearance of a spaceship over Route 135.

The issue of what it all meant was swirling around my thoughts when I met with Ralph and Dennis at springtime Powell Cemetery in the Old Quaker Burying Ground in Bethpage on April 22, 2013. On my way to them I had seen the second occurrence of an airplane not moving in the sky over the Seaford-Oyster Bay Expressway, as mentioned in Part II of this book.

The bulky, bearded gents from Central Islip, Ralph and Dennis, broke out an Ovilus from Ralph's worn brown leather satchel that looked like a doctor's bag.

The entrance to Powell Cemetery. It was here during the 2010 Long Island Devil Investigation that investigators said they experienced paranormal phenomena, including being touched, smelling scents, hearing voices, cries, and laughter, and seeing shadow people and ghosts. But is it the home of the alleged entity known as the Long Island Devil?

Paranormal Investigator Ralph DeMeyer holds an "Ovilus" spirit talking box, as his brother Dennis DeMeyer conducts and EVP session in the background at Powell Cemetery in Bethpage.

An Ovilus is a spirit talking box about the size of a bar of soap that says words in a 1970s robotic voice. Supposedly, the words it utters are chosen by the supernatural, but in actuality, the words had been physically imputed into a chip inside the box. The words are believed by many ghost hunters to be released in response to "trigger" frequencies inspired by the spirits. The thought is that the box can be used by spirits to convey messages. The user asks a question and then waits for an answer: "How long have you been dead?" a lot of ghost hunters like to ask, and then they turn to the box to listen for a response. Many of the responses are useless or sound mechanical to the point of being garbled.

The particular Ovilus Ralph took out of his paranormal doctor's bag and rested against the top of an old gray gravestone had 2,000 words or so burned into its chip, said Ralph. He believed the box to be an effective tool for the spirits to convey messages to us in real time. I had seen the box work effectively a few times and knew it could touch upon the door of the spirit world, but it never seemed to get much farther than that. I was curious if it could reach extraterrestrials, too.

A view inside lush Powell Cemetery. This graveyard is known to be haunted. It might also be a place visited occasionally by a lone extraterrestrial, if you believe the Long Island Devil is real.

By this point in my career as a ghost investigator and reporter of the paranormal, I had used an Ovilus several times in graveyards and had developed little faith in it actually serving as a conduit for the spirits. A few times it did produce words that weren't even burned into its chip, which raised eyebrows of ghost investigators present.

So, I let Ralph and Dennis do what they had secretly come for today, and that was ghost hunt, not to look for the Devil. I, on the other hand, had come to the graveyard to find the Long Island Devil, not ghosts. I must admit, I was disappointed that they were not interested in finding evidence of the all black creature that I was looking for; conversely, I sensed they were disappointed in me because I was barely interested in their methods for finding ghosts.

By now the late afternoon's pale sun had waned into cold pink and auburn pastel clouds in the frozen western sky. A shivering wind blew. It waved through the creaking branches of the ancient trees in the old cemetery. I searched the tops of the tallest pines, looking like primordial wizards against the blowing bruised clouds overhead, scrutinizing the cavernous dark spaces between their shaggy weeping-willow-like green boughs high up, where the Devil, if it exists, might hide sometimes, watching the world roll by, waiting for the mother ship to arrive. The branches of the stately trees swayed in old sage knowingness and swirled up in the frosty wind.

It was my belief that somewhere out there in the windswept trees of Long Island's thawing springtime woods of browns and greens, smelling of fresh earth, hid an unknown type of creature. Once again, the description says it all: midnight black with wings. Most interestingly, it wears a grim reaper-type cape and a hood and has the ability to teleport and disappears at will. If reports of it are true, it can fly.

Of course, it sounds just as nuts as believing that aliens in UFOs were contacting me or anybody else personally. But I had seen the UFOs of late. I had never seen the Long Island Devil face-to-face.

However, I believe the Devil did once swoop down off a utility wire thirty feet above the street and slice the air, whizzing past me like a sharp gust of wind. It happened during one of the many visits Diane and I made to the haunted graveyards in Bethpage, in 2010, to search for the monster, as some people might call it.

We believe that if the Devil does exist, it dwells in or often visits the graveyards of the Old Quaker Burying Ground when it comes out of the woods of Bethpage State Park and the parklands of storied Mount Misery. It might be invisible much of the time, we just don't know. I saw only a long black streak out of the corner of my eye when it whizzed by me. It moved inhumanly fast. I also heard the *whoosh* sound that its body made as it sleekly cut the dusk like a speeding missile, followed by one beat of what I believe was either its cape thrashing the wind or its large prehistoric bat-like wings flapping beside me.

By the time I turned my eyes to it, the Devil—or whatever it was that flew past me—was gone. The heavy utility wire hanging between poles at the edge of the graveyard, at the timid little street at the front of the cemetery, bounced wildly from the force of whatever jumped off it. The beast that pushed off that wire had significant weight and force. It flew right past me, but I barely caught a glimpse of it. I immediately turned on the video camera in my hand and recorded the bouncing wire and narrated what had just happened to me. But my report of "The Incredible Bouncing Wire" did not hold the power it would have had if I had recorded on video the actual black Devil flying around the graveyard like the Wicked Witch of the West on her broomstick in *The Wizard of Oz*.

When it came to the existence of this elusive creature, I was relying chiefly on stories told to me by people who actually saw the Long Island Devil. I believe these folks who gave me their reports to be sane. Some of these people signed releases, so I could tell their stories and use their actual names. Others were not as forthcoming and refused to allow me to use their names in connection to their stories. They did not want their identities known to anybody because they feared people would think they were crazy.

I still doubted myself about actually having witnessed such an unlikely event as an airplane hanging motionless in the sky, even after having seen it occur a second time.

Like the second sighting, the third time I saw this happen was in broad daylight on the loveliest of warm spring days in blossoming eastern Long Island. The date was April 26, 2013, only four days after I met with Ralph and Dennis. On this day the reality of an alien presence in my life was solidified in my thinking once and for all, absolutely, and for certain.

50

Third appearance of spaceship over Eastern Long Island

On that sunny, gorgeous, spring day, I was driving the company's "gold" minivan east under a bright yellow sun on dusty, old Route 25 in Calverton. I had already driven past enormous Calverton National Cemetery on the left and the tiny Grumman Memorial Park on the right. Grumman Memorial Park is where two of the jets Grumman made for the military during the Cold War years are displayed in memory of all the Grumman employees who built them. Of course, that's before the company was acquired by Northrop and moved off Long Island. The Memorial is the spot where people claim to see groups of ghosts walking in front of the park, possibly coming from the cemetery. Some people say they think the ghosts belong to former Grumman workers who were buried at Calverton National Cemetery and gather sometimes at the memorial.

This section of Route 25 has always been known as a haunted road. As I drove under the bright sun, the land opened up into vast brown farmlands on my left under a luscious sapphire sky. Then I saw it: a glinting silver oddity pasted in the sky over a farm. It was a cigar-shaped craft, looking like it was moving slightly up and down rather than horizontally. It remained essentially in place. At first, I thought it was a balloon, then I thought it might be a blimp, then I resigned myself to experiencing another alien craft visitation.

As if magically, as I looked up at the craft, I knew for certain I was in for another episode of "Another Airplane Hanging Silently in the Sky." It was a show produced solely for me. I could only imagine the purpose of this newest performance: it was for my continued edification via the aliens—or I had snapped mentally without knowing it and I was now insane?

In this case, the craft did not appear to be much bigger than a car. It was nothing like the jumbo jet glued in the sky over the dark streets of Garden City on that woebegone night of the CE-5 meeting in the graveyard. This craft might have been the size of a private jet. It was about a quarter mile in the sky over the farm, which is not considered very high up for an airplane.

Not again! I thought.

It had been less than a week since I saw a similar sight over the Seaford-Oyster Bay Expressway on my way to meet Ralph and Dennis to investigate Powell Cemetery for signs of the Long Island Devil.

I felt embarrassed and totally self conscious when I thought to myself that another mysterious craft was appearing to me for another mysterious reason. Unlike the two other times I had witnessed planes not moving in the sky, this time, as I looked up at it, I saw it was moving, but barely.

Meanwhile, traffic was thick as fleas on Route 25 at this hour. People were busy traveling to places out on eastern Long Island for their businesses, mixed with people taking advantage of the gentle springtime afternoon, the trees just starting to sprout green leaves, the grass in the fields just beginning to turn deep green. The time was 2:30 p.m. I was driving through the glorious fresh day minding my own business when it happened. There it was.

The heavy traffic worked to my advantage because the cars and trucks on this road moved so slowly, for whatever reason, that I was afforded a constant view of the craft. I thought of the UFO as a "spaceship" because it didn't have the shape of an airplane. There were no wings or a tail that I could see. I saw no exhaust from engines. There was no landing gear that I could make out. If it had been an airplane, the only way I would be able to explain it flying so low to the ground is that it had just taken off from one of the small local airports or was planning to land at one. If that was the case, however, where was the landing gear? It was not a dirigible (blimp) and it was not a crop duster. It was not a balloon or a kite. Rather, it was a classic cigar-shaped UFO, the likes of which had been seen often around the world for many decades. I had seen this sort of craft over the Long Island Sound when Diane and I were returning from Vermont on the Port Jefferson Ferry, but that cigar-shaped space vehicle was unbelievably large, maybe the size of Lake Ronkonkoma.

Of course, I had to laugh to myself about this latest showing of an alien presence. I hoped I wasn't the only person out of all the hundreds of people traveling that road in that area of Long Island at that time who observed the craft. But I could certainly understand why the attention of the other people on the road might have been focused on the sight of the recently tilled rich brown earth of the open farm, and not what was above it, because the land was beautiful to the eyes. Yes, I think I was the only person on the road at that time who noticed it or who showed an interest.

Slowly I traveled eastward, keeping my eyes on the stationary craft until I was lined up with it—it hovering high over farm to my left. I was now parked just outside the farm and across the dusty road on the shoulder with my eyes turned towards the craft. The enormous blue sky with big puffy white clouds in the background became a viewing screen, like a chalkboard. The lesson written on the chalkboard was intended to serve as yet another validation that extraterrestrials were showing their spaceships to me. My head was turned out the open window.

How could this be happening? I thought. Of course, I was excited by the possibility that this could be real and also so personal, but I was terrified that I was subject to the whims of a life form the likes of which I could not even imagine. What did they want with me?

I observed the craft for about five minutes. It moved at a nearly imperceptible creep but not really in any one direction. No airplanes that I knew of could possibly move so slowly. Maybe the Navy and Air Force had classified jets in Afghanistan, like the old Harriers, that could hover like helicopters. But no planes over the farmlands of eastern Long Island would be so sophisticated.

The craft had barely moved a few thousand feet over and away from the farm by the time I decided to leave the area. There was no sound coming from it. Remember, it was low in the sky and not far away, so I had a clear view of it. There was not much about it to describe. It was silver and shaped like a cigar. There were no ropes attached to it—of this I am certain. Sometimes it caught the sun as it wobbled occasionally and, at those times, it shone silver, otherwise it was dull like pewter. I searched for reasons to believe it was some kind of weather balloon or a kite or some other object. But it was too high to be something connected to the ground, like a kite or balloon, and there was nothing in the sky showing it was attached to anything. Moreover, it was too big to be a balloon.

"I have to go," I spoke to the craft. Maybe the aliens heard me, maybe not.

I only left the area because I could tell if I stayed where I was parked on the side of the busy road, somebody was going to slam into the back of the minivan. The company I work for would never understand why I was sitting on the side of the road in Calverton watching a UFO float above a farm, when I should have been on my way to Riverhead to collect three developmentally disabled individuals to bring them back to their home in Ridge where I worked. I didn't want to have to explain any of this to my manager, so I took off, wondering if the UFO was going to follow me or appear to me again before I got to Riverhead to collect the people I was supposed to pick up. Or would they beam me up to the spacecraft for an examination and DNA collection?

As I drove away on the black, dusty road, I couldn't help but remember what psychics who participated in the Long Island Devil Investigation of 2010 insisted: that all forty or so people who were involved in the investigation were there because they were called by higher forces, chosen to be given secretive knowledge. "It's no accident that we are here," I recalled one of the psychics stating. "It was meant to happen."

At the time, I thought it was a quaint notion to believe that I and the other investigators were hand-chosen by God or the spirits or aliens or some other kind of great entity to gather together to investigate the Long Island Devil, as if by some special invitation from benevolents that really cared. But now the words the psychics had spoken back then had my undivided attention because I wondered if the Long Island Devil was really an extraterrestrial and all this was tied up together, leading to some ultimate purpose that I could not see.

Was I supposed to pursue all this as an education that would be required for something in the future? Perhaps I would need it for some kind of mission? I wondered if extraterrestrials had the power to orchestrate such an event as getting forty people who were of interest to them to join together to experience something they otherwise would not have experienced, maybe so they could tell others about it and teach them in preparation for the great alien Coming. What would be the intent of such an orchestration? It would be to get us prepared to meet our new masters or new intergalactic friends.

So many lines had become blurred in my life within the last two months. I knew I had stumbled onto a secret that was both amazing and profound, but I couldn't understand any of its relevance.

A lack of relevance has always been a problem with understanding ghosts, too. Ghosts often appear to people who can not understand the relevance of the strange ghostly appearances to their own lives.

The hunch I was developing was that aliens from other planets don't think like we do because they are life forms that are radically unlike us, and thus they can not relate to our needs, hopes, and experiences.

Aliens certainly have their own incomprehensible agendas. Perhaps they are taking over our planet and this is how they do it. They show their ships to people first, warm them up to the idea, then *bang!*, we are made to submit to them as their slaves. Who knows?

Maybe soon they'd be directing humankind to strip the world's resources, so it can all be transported to their world by way of an Einstein-Rosen Bridge, a wormhole. Obviously, if aliens are on Earth, then anything is possible, including an alien invasion without it seeming like an alien invasion.

At any rate, on the way back from Riverhead I passed the farm where the flying cigar was hovering in the sky a half-hour earlier, but it was no longer there. I grew a little afraid at the second because I felt for certain I had been visited again.

Why?

It was on this exact day that I got into an extended e-mail conversation with an editor at *FATE* magazine. Jamie grabbed my attention when she talked about the great "shift" that occurred within mankind's thinking in 2011.

To me, "the great shift" was something I read about in New Age magazines and on the Internet. I always thought it was "out there" type thinking. But now I thought over the words she wrote to me about a great shift taking place in everyone's thinking, and realized I had to look deeper into this because the great shift might be alien inspired.

Jamie is the editor who Phyllis Gaulde, the publisher of *FATE*, directed to edit a story by me and Diane called, "Are UFOs Overtaking Long Island, New York?" The lengthy article was going into a special UFO Issue. Also, in the same issue was a second story I wrote about my experience with CE-5 and the appearance of airplanes that hung silently in the sky, but were really spaceships. The title of my second article was "Close Encounters of the 5th Kind."

I reviewed the things the kindly editor wrote in her e-mails, soon believing her words were part of the puzzle the aliens were laying out in front of me and perhaps many other people. The words were meant for my eyes, or at least I was beginning to believe nothing was an accident any more, that all things are linked and connected and have meaning in relationship to each other. Everything has relevance somehow to the viewer's life. Our trouble as humans is we just have problems seeing it.

I didn't know if you would call this a newfound "faith" in something greater than me in the universe, but clearly there appeared to be some kind of purpose behind the abstract alien messages I was receiving.

But what did any of it mean? And who or what was sending the messages?

The world was turning upside down for me. Naturally, I was afraid of how far I'd go with all this. It was turning into such a bizarre, strange world.

On the other hand, I was growing evermore fascinated in the development of my alien education, the primer to which was being bestowed upon me by members of a civilization from across the heavens, I now believed.

Finally, I had seen with my own eyes what so many other people throughout the decades of the twentieth century—and for more than 10,000 years—have been claiming to see, and have carved petroglyphs of and painted pictorials on cave walls about—that spaceships have been flying in our skies forever and appear to all the peoples of the world, regardless of location, culture, or ethnicity.

Such images are etched not only on rocks around the world, but also on 100 square miles of the Nazca Plain in the arid desert of sweltering Peru. There we find testimony from hundreds of years ago that Indians of that area, who are now gone, invited aliens down to commune. The natives made images of creatures that can only be seen from the sky. Do the images point to landing strips for alien crafts, as some people think, or did the natives of the land just decide one morning to go out into the burning sun and kill a few upcoming years by making precise images of creatures that can only be seen from the sky so birds have something to look at as they fly by? Such is unlikely. One immense image the natives created appears to be a being in a space suit.

Why some people see spaceships and aliens while others do not is a mystery.

I was beginning to think my alien education was also an invitation to glimpse a more intelligent life form visiting Earth. I was convinced the purpose of my education, while still to be determined, came about as the result of asking to meet and greet extraterrestrials through a CE-5 meditation.

Be careful if you are intrigued to go out to a graveyard at night and call aliens down to visit you on Earth. The jury is still out as to the meaning of it all. It could prove fatal or angelic.

*

To be honest, I didn't know why the sighting of the orange glowing spaceship over the Long Island Sound in August of 2012 while on the Port Jefferson Ferry clicked something in my brain that threw my attention so completely to UFOs. At the time, I was fully occupied with the study of ghosts. Back on that night when Diane and I saw the enormous spacecraft, I knew in an instant I was meant to pursue them. It wasn't long before I signed up for a brand new CE-5 meet-up group on Long Island and joined MUFON members at meetings. I never had much of a passion for pursing UFOs before I saw the orange craft over the Sound.

I mean, ever since I saw the burning craft on the day of the Great New York Blackout of 1965, I thought spaceships were up there in our skies, and that people really saw them, but I never considered pursuing them. Sometimes at my lectures with Diane as *The Paranormal Adventurers* I felt embarrassed for people who raised their hands during discussion time and said they saw UFOs or that they had been visited by aliens in the night. It happened more often than you might think in the 500 or so lectures we gave since 2005. As a ghost investigator, my chief interest was always ghostly phenomena, which I firmly believe in because I saw ghosts, heard them, and felt their presences for myself. When people in our audiences told us about their UFO experiences, I'd cringe inside because I didn't want audience members to get side-tracked in our discussion of ghosts and concentrate on UFOs, which many people who are on the fence about ghosts absolutely don't believe in and don't want to hear about. Oddly, I have come to realize spaceships appear to some people and not others, just like ghosts appear to some people and not others. Why is this?

I think it was this very question that led me to want to know more about extraterrestrials and their history. I wanted to learn more about the reason why ghosts and aliens have so much in common. To deny the possibility of either is understandable, but all people owe it to themselves to at least look into the spirit world and into what generals, pilots, and many other people are saying about UFOs.

Have aliens genetically altered some families of human beings so they are receptive to visitors from other worlds? Is this what extraterrestrials do in their spaceships to people—take semen from men and eggs from women and splice into the DNA their own codes? There is a growing movement sweeping across the planet that believes we have been genetically altered many thousands of years ago by aliens, so that we became separate from other animals on this planet.

Remember an earlier discussion of Janet Russell? She's the Long Island psychic who said she was taken aboard a spacecraft and shown fetuses of humans crossbred with aliens in glass jars. Remember her comments about the creation of new technologies that have been invented in just the last fifty years? Is she right? Have aliens stepped up their DNA splicing during that time?

Is it true that beings from other planets are going to one day announce themselves and appear over the skies of the world as many people think? Do their appearances to individuals prepare the human race for the inevitable meeting? It will be the most profound event in human history. Will I be one of the people who will be introducing the aliens to humans? Was I chosen because I explore the unknown or because I'm a writer and lecturer?

A big question related to all this is whether aliens are already manipulating us through brainwashing or through undetectable ongoing transmissions in radio waves, or though some kind of drug in our water, the likes of which pacifies us to perform certain tasks that benefit them, not us.

One morning, in the summer of 2012, I felt a rough little bump on my chest where it meets my left shoulder. I ran my fingers over it and felt it was not part of my body. It was hard and solidly black. Because I live in a semi-rural area with lots of trees and vegetation, I immediately suspected a deer tick had attached itself to me. They are everywhere on Long Island, especially out east where I live. In the past I had to pry them out of my skin. This happened several times over the years.

I studied the black object in the bathroom mirror before I lobbed Vaseline on it and waited for the tick to climb out of my skin so it could get air and breathe. I waited a long time, but it never moved. If it was a tick, then I had to suppose it was dead because the Vaseline smothered it, or it died from my poking at it with my fingers—or maybe it just died on its own.

I took a pair of tweezers and removed the small black item from my flesh. It had a long slim tail, as if it was designed to be inserted into flesh. A red mark lay on the skin underneath the spot where the black thing was inserted. I examined the item under a magnifying glass and saw the round top was composed of some kind of fabric made up of minuscule squares. It was definitely not a tick. The edges of it were slightly red, possibly from clinging to the flesh and absorbing traces of blood. I figured maybe it was a material that clung to me or stuck in me when I turned my shoulder over in bed. Perhaps it was tree material like a leaf that somehow found its way into my sheets. So I went up to my room and checked the sheets; they were clean. I didn't see any material around the bed that might have flaked onto the sheets.

I had to suddenly disregard the notion that I had brought an outside material into my bed when I realized that I had fallen out of bed the night before. I remembered this fact in an instant, but I hadn't remembered a thing about it until that second. I stood over my bed and looked at the shape of clothes on a rack next to the bed staring back at me.

Maybe when I fell out of bed the night before my shoulder banged into something and a piece of it lodged into my flesh. I stood still in the hallway staring at the wallpaper, remembering this event, which I had not remembered up to just a moment before in the bedroom. I had not fallen out of bed in twenty years. The time I did fall out of bed twenty years ago was only as a result of drinking too much at a party and turning over in my bed, only to roll out of it like an idiot.

Now, in a flash, I had a memory of falling out of bed just the night before. On this occasion, I had neither drunk nor done any drugs. I also suddenly remembered the face of an eagle or some other kind of bird from a dream I had at the time I fell out of bed. It was a strange dream, as most of mine are; I remembered some talking, but I don't know what was being said, or by whom. As I thought about it, I recalled a little girl with an old woman's face with sunglasses on and bright blonde hair in a bun on her head.

I shuddered at all this and dropped the black thing from my shoulder into a clean glass jar, several of which I keep handy in the kitchen to store extra pasta sauce when I make a lot of it.

This was turning out to be a bleak day for me, because I feared there was more to this black thing and the dream and the falling out of bed episode than met the eye. I didn't want to know what happened.

It gave me the creeps to look at the black thing, the size and shape of a black clove used for baking hams, sitting at the bottom of the glass jar. It reminded me of the fetuses Janet Russell saw in the glass jars when she claims a chip was implanted in her arm. She felt the chip was intended to track her.

Had I been implanted with a chip? Have *you* dear reader? Has this happened to you, too?

Was this thing in my shoulder an alien chip? It was so thin and insignificant I would imagine most people who receive such an implantation probably just brush it off as a strange tick or something, and as it goes deeper into the flesh, perhaps concern about it lessens because the alien instructions it uploads says to ignore it.

Then I wondered if I had removed the chip out of my skin before it did its job of uploading its programs into my brain? Or had it already done its brainwashing work and was not any longer needed by the aliens? If I had not touched it, would it have sunk deeper and deeper into my skin until it infiltrated my bloodstream?

Or was it just a strange piece of fabric that pressed into my flesh because it was in my bed? Maybe it became lodged in my skin when I fell out of bed. Who was the old woman with sunglasses watching me in my dreams?

"I fell out of bed?" The words didn't feel right to me.

Now, I hope you see the strange kinds of things that were and still are happening to me. They are the kind of things one questions, but never finds answers. They seemed to be pieces of a puzzle I was invited to piece together, but I'm not permitted to see that puzzle completed in its entirety.

Can you sense the odd flavors of my experiences, neither dark and overtly sinister, nor happy and insightful? Can you detect the queerness of it all, like walking into the fun house at an amusement park where the red lights flash and swirl in your eyes and clowns jump out of the walls?

Either I was now crazy or I was actually experiencing these things. Was I becoming like people in mental institutions who claimed aliens visit them during the night and take them aboard spaceships? I couldn't help holding the thought in the back of my mind that the night before, when I fell out of bed, I had an encounter with a life form I didn't understand. It was all so foggy, like the windswept Long Island bays before a morning storm.

There is probably no way aliens can communicate directly with us using their mouths, if they have any. Certainly, it must be done telepathically, but I'm guessing these life forms are probably so vastly different than us that there is no perfect way of ever meeting minds with them. They do things in ways that are strange to us, and visa verse.

I sealed the top to the glass jar I was using to hold the black chip. In the jar was also a small piece of tissue paper that I used to handle the black fragment from my shoulder. Then I left it for months. In the glass jar a white mold has grown. The mold looks like a ball of thin cotton. I don't know if this is the result of the black item or the tissue. The glass jar was washed clean before I used it, but I can't rule out the mold coming from a residue of sauce. I'm almost positive this is not the case. Coincidentally, the black object grew slightly larger over that time, too. If and when it's necessary, and I have the funds to do it, I will have a lab examine the material. I won't open the jar till then.

I'm almost afraid to find out what the black thing is.

*

One Saturday night after I returned home from work at about 9:30, I spent a few minutes tidying up and then looked out my side door window to see if a whistling type noise I heard outside was Diane arriving in her car to spend the night with me. Upon inspection, the noise I heard must have been a car's engine whining as it moved down the dark street in front of my little white house, or some other kind of noise emitted from someone's house down the street. At that time, I noticed how beautifully bright the moon was in the night sky. It was a full moon and intensely white.

I turned from the door and went back to preparing for Diane's arrival. Turns out she was later than usual, and I found myself going back and forth to the door window, looking out to see if she had arrived in my driveway yet. In the meantime, I kept hearing odd noises, like whistles and clanking sounds. I was getting worried about Diane, and I couldn't call her cell phone because she had it turned off. Each of the times I went to the door I was startled by the white intensity of the full moon. At one point I stayed at the door and just stared at the moon for a long time through the trees. I felt oddly comforted, even pleased to do so.

Finally, I moved away from the window and sat on the couch. Shortly, I heard Diane's car horn in my driveway. I went to the door and looked out the window. I saw her coming up the path towards my house, but I did not see the bright moon any longer.

I stepped outside and looked around. The moon was in the opposite area of the sky from where I had seen it earlier. And it was lower in the sky and only a quarter moon. That night a helicopter with burning lights flew over my house.

What had I been looking at in the sky over my house? Was it a spaceship? Did it upload a file to my brain while it was there?

*

Months earlier, in late 2012, I lectured alone at the Hillside Branch of the Queens library. I was speaking solo about UFOs. I booked a few libraries to see how people would react to a discussion about UFOs. The name of the program was "Are Spaceships Visiting Long Island and New York City?"

I sent out fliers to about thirty libraries, but only four responded, indicating a very low interest in the subject. Hillside Library was my first lecture of my solo spaceship program. About thirty people attended. They were all adults. There were three men who sat in the back. They looked like they were wearing government issued shoes and windbreakers. They did not ask any questions or make any comments. They simply stared at me through the whole lecture. Several people in the audience told personal stories of UFOs. The three silent men in the back never took their eyes off me.

A month later, I gave a lecture at the Shirley-Mastic-Moriches Community Library in Mastic. This is UFO country. The library is located just down the road from infamous Southold Park, where a spaceship allegedly crashed in 1992. And Moriches Bay is just down the opposite end of the road where some people claimed aliens were killed when government helicopters shot down their craft in 1989. Right down the William Floyd Parkway south from the Library is Smith Point Beach. It was ten miles out from the beach on July 1996 that TWA Flight 800 exploded over Moriches Bay, killing 230 people, and witnessed by hundreds of people on the beach.

The lecture at the Mastic library was booked as a Young Adult program and attended by only a handful of high school students who stared at me with open mouths as I spoke. They didn't know what to make of me. They thought they were in for a cute UFO show; instead, they got warnings to watch out for the invading spaceship people. Though it was a teen program, adults also showed up. One man stayed after the program ended. He was in the company of a woman. I think she might have been a doctor, a psychiatrist. He told me he had been abducted. They were both very serious. He was shaking as he told me.

People often confide in me about things they would never talk about to most other people. I remember a library director in Queens named Scott who told me for several nights in a row he and his cousins spied a UFO hovering over the trees in the woodlands of Pennsylvania. He was young at the time. The experience meant a lot to him because he was awakened to the alien presence on Earth. He ended up being a participant in the Long Island Devil Investigation. He invited me and Diane to speak about ghosts at different libraries where he was the director and we spoke several times at these libraries. I met his mother and father because they came to the programs, too.

Probably one of the most alarming first-hand accounts I have come across is from a man who would never grant me permission to tell his story using his name. He is still afraid of what he saw and experienced afterwards, and is afraid of government retaliation. The man is from the Brentwood area of Suffolk County, though his story is from another interesting area.

The man said the year was 1999, and he was standing guard at night on a Navy ship that transported Marines to places where they were needed. The ship was empty at this time. It was performing maneuvers called "alligator squares" in an area somewhere off Florida, in the infamous Bermuda Triangle, also known as Devil's Triangle. The "Triangle" is about 800 square miles of water in the Atlantic where many ships and airplanes have gone missing. The ship this sailor was on could house 2,000 Marines at one time, if they needed to be transported to a battle zone in a hurry. He pointed out that most people don't realize that the U.S. Marines are part of the U.S. Navy.

The Navy grunt was stationed at night alone on the starboard side of the ship as it covered large swathes of the Triangle. He had a radio and a log. He kept timely notes of things he was required to observe. It was a clear, warm night, and the sea was gentle. There was also a sailor stationed port side, as well as one on the bow and another aft. Thus, the skies and water on all sides of the ship were being watched.

Then a light appeared in the clear, starry night sky. The light broke apart into three distinct lights and they separated to form a triangle in the sky.

The sailor on starboard—let's call him Ishmael—wrote in his log that a star split apart into three parts and formed a triangle. The parts hung in the sky, then swirled around the sky, and then went back to forming a single point of light.

Just then the radio buzzed. The sailor standing guard at port asked the other guards on watch if they saw what he saw, a light split apart and then form a triangle overhead. All but the man on the bow saw it because he was the man at the front of the ship facing frontward while all the action had occurred behind him.

When the tour of duty for the night was over, and the four men were relieved, they were summonsed into a room where stood an officer, the captain, and two men in suits. The men observed the sailors, sat them down, and stared at them. An officer asked them what they saw out there on their tour. "Well sir," began the first sailor who was asked, and he turned to his log to report what he had witnessed.

"No, I don't want your log. I want to know what you saw," insisted the officer.

"Sir," said my friend, when he was asked, "I recorded in my log..."

"I know about your log, here, give me that book, you'll get a new one... I want to know what did you see? I'm asking you what you know for certain you saw out there tonight. You didn't see anything, isn't that right?"

The sailors looked at one another, desperate to say the right thing so they could get out of this room safely and resume their lives. They knew what they were supposed to say, so they said it: "No, sir. We didn't see anything."

"That's what I thought," said the officer. The captain looked to the two men in suits and nodded.

One of the civilian men stepped up to the light so that it was on only half of his face. He was a hard-looking man. "You will never speak about this, not even to your wife. You will not talk about it with even your best friends. You shall never discuss it with each other. Do you understand? Are we clear?"

"Yes, sir," said Ishmael, feeling like he had been stepped on.

When days later he was finally back at his apartment on dry land after the ship's maneuvers were over, he'd look out his window frequently because he thought he saw cars with cop types in them, like Feds, sitting outside his apartment. He grew concerned for his safety. When he talked to his best friend on the phone, who was coincidentally the sailor who stood guard at port side on the night of the triangle lights, his friend refused to articulate on the phone anything but grunts in response to questions Ishmael asked, like, "Do you think we're being watched?"

PART V

CHAPTER NINE

CALLING ALL EXTRATER- RESTRIALS

51

"Let's Talk."

I was off from work on a Tuesday in late April, 2013. It was a perfectly mild, sunny spring day and I was in love with life. An excitement was building all around in the form of sprouting red and purple flowers, green plants, and yellow bushes bursting with color, with trees turning rapidly greener. I drove up to Cedar Beach in Mount Sinai and parked in front of the placid blue Long Island Sound. Large, puffy clouds billowed by in the far west.

"Okay, aliens," I said, looking out my windshield at the wide vista of the blue sky over the Sound. "I'm ready, come and show yourselves to me. Let's talk."

I waited. I waited some more. A woman in a black sweatshirt sat down on the sand near the water with her brown dog. A couple got out of their shiny, red car and sat on the rocky tan sand of the beach at the edge of the parking lot, looking out at the blue water. No spaceships. I was actually surprised none showed up.

April blended into tender May.

Diane and I gave a presentation to a seniors club in Glen Cove. The Centre Club was well represented, with about a hundred and twenty people in attendance. Unlike any other lecture we've ever given, this was only twenty minutes long and we didn't charge a fee. The voice of the woman who called us and invited us to speak had a voice similar to my mother's voice, and when I heard it I was immediately happy to support her group in any way I could. I miss my mom. I knew I could easily convince Diane to speak before the group because she's a pushover when it comes to helping people. The club program director, Ms. Dorothy Williams, had gotten our name from the Glen Cove Public Library. We had spoken at the library many times over our eight years of lecturing.

When the May 2, 2013 lecture in Glen Cove was over, after Mrs. Williams presented us with a certificate of appreciation in a glass frame and photos were taken, Diane and I drove back to her house in West Hempstead. From there I got in my SUV and drove to work in the Pine Barrens. I had to be at work by 5 p.m.

52

Military Overtakes Rocky Point Preserve.

A helicopter circles the Pine Barrens. Such visits by helicopters are common in the Pine Barrens. But what are authorities looking for?

I was not at my worksite long when the thuds of a heavy helicopter, a military type, cut the air above the house where I work. I was out in the yard, so I witnessed it doing a slow flyover right above me and the trees. In my vehicle I had a camera ready for just such an event and I had prepared it for when the helicopter should come back. The helicopter circled the area in a wide circumference, sometimes dipping so low on the horizon that I lost sight of it in between the branches of trees. It stayed in the area about twenty-five minutes, and then vanished.

The climax to all this madness that I'm describing, the grand total culmination and sum of all the parts I have presented to you thus far, took place on Saturday, May 4, 2013.

This sunny spring day found me standing outside my regular work place in the heart of the Pine Barrens of Ridge. Literally, directly across the narrow country street from my workplace, is an endless wall of pine forest. This wall runs along the edge of over 5,000 acres of the Rocky Point Preserve, land owned by the state and jealously guarded by the DEC.

I stood on the black tar street, looking through the trees as multiple military helicopters circled the Pine Barrens. They sometimes flew over the house and circled around it. What were they looking for? Me? Were they searching for a spaceship that stayed in close proximity to me? Were they looking for aliens on the grounds that were watching me or Men in Black following me?

At one point I looked up at a passing helicopter low to the tree line. It was carrying a truck by cables. The helicopter was loud and low to the trees. Another helicopter circled around, too. The second helicopter was big and painted in camouflage designs.

Then, as I watched this activity swirling around me, wondering if I was somehow connected to all of it, I suddenly saw a soldier in a military uniform driving a one-man quad. It was a machine made for a single man to ride in rough terrain. Behind him appeared a long line of military jeeps. They rolled up the quiet country road like killers, pale riders into a fight. The roars of the vehicles contradicted the serene peace of the woods and birds scattered as the thunder of helicopter blades overhead grew louder.

Each of the ten or so military vehicles that passed me were staffed fully with soldiers in dark uniforms, but I could not tell from what branch of the military they were from for I saw no insignias. The vehicles had no insignias on them, either. There were no stars on the hoods or words like "U.S. Army" displayed on the doors. There was nothing to identify these soldiers or their vehicles. They had no identity. This was just like the helicopters, which were either black or painted camouflage.

Were these the soldiers from the secret Anti-UFO Army? Were they members of an army that is dedicated to protecting the public from the harm the aliens would cause us if they were allowed to roam freely? Was the Anti-UFO Army present in the Pine Barrens to shoot out of the sky spaceships and then kill the extraterrestrials that should survive? Why were military helicopters carrying equipment into the Pine Barrens? I had never seen the military in the woods here before. Why were soldiers occupying the woods? These woods are supposed to be dedicated to recreation for New York State residents; the woods had never been the site of Army games.

I knew in my gut this was the real deal. The Anti-UFO Army was onto something and they were going to flush it out of the woods, kill it, and then deny it all. My chief concern was whether or not I was the reason the aliens were nearby to begin with.

Of course, I was on the clock at work while I saw all this activity. A fellow employee named Lori, who lives near this spot, told me that earlier, before she came to work, she felt the ground rumbling and saw the shades over her bedroom windows shaking from a thunderous helicopter's mighty blades thudding across the low sky as it swooped over her house on the way to the woods around our work place. "What's going on?" she asked. I recorded what she told me on video so people would believe me about all this.

I was prepared now, too. I had a video camera ready.

As the helicopters flew by, I video recorded them carrying equipment back and forth into the woods. It took three hours of waiting, but I also caught the military convoy rolling back down the little road in front of where I work. The sun was going down. I had figured the soldiers would probably not stay in the woods in the dark because it would require the Anti-UFO Army to set up tents and latrines, and provide food and other services to the soldiers. It was a lot more practical to send them back to a base to eat and sleep. Five vehicles exited the woods and rolled past me. Only about half of the vehicles that went into the woods earlier were now coming out. Where were the others?

I surely looked like a goofball as I waved to the soldiers to get their attention so they wouldn't have the presence of mind to figure out that the object sitting on top of the mailbox in front of the house in which I worked was actually a video camera that was turned on and was currently recording their every move.

It was so important to me that I document this military activity in the Pine Barrens. It had been going on all spring. The Pine Barrens have long been the focus of spaceships and the Anti-UFO Army, if you believe the stories. The video came out clear. I now have a copy of this video and photos, and my story of UFOs over Long Island in safe keeping so that if anything should happen to me—like I'm killed or abducted—the information will be released to newspapers.

Later that evening, as the workers in the house where I work were gathered together to prepare to go home after taking care of all the tasks required for the residents, we talked as a group in the living room about the helicopters and the passing convoy of trucks. We all agreed that it was highly unusual for such activity to take place in woods where local residents are not allowed to even walk without a permit from the DEC. A few of the employees scoured their cell phones for Internet information on what was going on, but no information was found, nothing on Channel 12 Long Island News either and nothing in *Newsday*, the island's only daily newspaper. This reminded me of Carmela Somma saying that when the UFO was shot down over Moriches Bay in 1989, nobody could drive south of Montauk Highway in Center Moriches. And even though Center

Moriches had been under Martial Law for two days, and military and police personnel were everywhere, there was not a lick of information ever reported in the local newspapers or on television.

53

Silenced?

At 9 p.m., our shift at the house was over and it was time to go home.

I walked to my car in the darkness of the strange night. It was parked at the edge of the property near the tree line where the state forest began. As I looked up at the stars, I heard helicopters and then detected noises from the woods. It sounded like people moving around on foot. The woods in the area have a healthy population of deer and other animals, so I didn't pay much attention until I saw a flashlight glint briefly in the trees located about a hundred feet from me. I was being watched.

As I flew down the road to get out of the area, the narrow road was suddenly clogged by a new convoy of military vehicles. They approached me from the only exit out of the area. I feared they were going to arrest me and confiscate my vehicle, bring me someplace to interrogate me. They had turned off Whiskey Road and then down the country road where I work. These vehicles were far more sinister in nature than the Jeeps I had seen earlier. They were painted camouflage and were bigger than the vehicles I video recorded. These humvees had gun turrets on top, though I did not see any guns or soldiers occupying the turrets. I had to steer my SUV to the extreme side of the road so there would be enough room for the military vehicles to pass.

I made a right onto Whiskey Road and aimed for my home in Rocky Point. As I did, a helicopter swooped over the tree line and the road above me. A sudden bright beam of light blinded me as the helicopter shot past and circled into the trees. When I got home, I waited for Diane to arrive, for she often stays with me overnight on weekends.

We sat on the couch in my living room and spent a good deal of time talking about everything that was going on. I hadn't yet informed her of the daily strange events happing in my life since I participated in CE-5. She sat stone-faced listening, stunned by the things I told her. As we spoke, a helicopter came visiting my residence, flying overhead and around my neighborhood. Diane and I went outside to watch it pass. It seemed the helicopter was pursuing something in the sky, for there was the shape of something a hundred feet in the air above it.

ABOVE: Military vehicles pass in a convoy on a lonely country road in the Pine Barrens of the Rocky Point Preserve where Joseph Flammer works. On this day, helicopters were circling around the area, also carrying equipment over the trees, including trucks.
BELOW: To back up his claims that he actually saw all this military activity in the Rocky Point Preserve, Mr. Flammer made sure he appeared in the video he shot of the trucks rolling out of the Pine Barrens. He is walking in the right side of the photograph.

The helicopter would be returning over and over again during the night, always with this other craft above it.

Diane looked scared. I was so sorry I had involved her. But somebody had to know, and she was the only person I could trust with this information, with my life. I didn't know if I was going to be pursued by the Anti-UFO Army, and maybe be silenced like John Ford was silenced, or if the aliens were coming directly for me.

Which was worse?

I would soon find out that having your house broken into in the middle of the night as you lay in bed and hear your front door forced open would be about the worst thing I'd want to experience short of being taken against my will into a spaceship.

54

Something Bangs Open
Front Door at 3:30 a.m. Help!

What broke into Joseph Flammer's front door while he and Diane slept at 3:30 in the morning? Was it meant to serve as a message telling him to stop investigating and writing about UFOs over Long Island? If so, who did it?

Diane and I could barely pull ourselves out of my comfortable bed at 10 a.m. on Sunday morning, September 8, 2013. It was a perfectly beautiful late summer day with puffy, white clouds floating overhead in a lazy summer sky the color of a baby's blue eyes. It had been a weird summer. Many strange things happened that I could not explain, many of which I have not listed in this book because there is just not enough space. These were things I had never experienced before.

On this glorious day, Diane and I would attend a paranormal investigation at Camp Hero State Park in Montauk with members of *Eastern Suffolk Paranormal* (ESP) and other good friends. I was excited to go on this adventure. Peggy Vetrano of ESP and I talked about doing this for over a year.

Diane and I felt tired and wished we could still sleep. We were exhausted because someone or something had broken into my house during the night as we slept. We were awakened by much noise. This happened at 3:45 in the morning, only five hours before we had to wake up to go to Camp Hero.

A tremendous *BOOM!* shook the small white dormer where we slept in an upstairs bedroom. Something crashed through the screen door at the front of the house and knocked open the heavy wooden door, causing the door to fly wide open.

On review, I saw the screen in the screen door hung limply inside of the door, meaning someone or something pushed right through the screen from outside.

There was not a breeze to be found that night, so the violent occurrence was not the result of a strong wind or a branch that fell against the house. In the many years I had lived in my home, nothing like this had ever happened. The old house is located on a dark and quiet street in the dusty hills of Rocky Point. It's the kind of street without sidewalks and the mail person pulls the truck up to a mailbox across the street when delivering the mail.

Of course, we jumped up in reaction to the frightful noise, with our hearts pounding in our throats. At the second it happened, I admit, I suspected alien beings were floating downstairs in my living room, ready to carry us off to the spaceship where they'd do things to us against our wills, like pack our insides with some kind of silvery medical instruments that read information about what we eat and about our sex lives and genes. Or maybe instead of aliens, solders from the Anti-UFO Army were in full black-ops attire and were busting into the house to arrest me for my involvement with aliens, though I didn't really have any involvement with aliens. It was all a one-sided deal I'd have to tell them. I doubt they would believe me, since they spend so much time chasing spaceships around my house.

I flew down the stairs to find the front door wide open. The screen in the screen door was down. It had been a sudden and violent assault on my home.

I went slowly through the rooms on the first floor, looking for evidence of an intruder, while Diane stayed in the bedroom upstairs, a cell phone in her tight hand, waiting for a shout from me to call the police. But I found no evidence of an intruder. There was also no sign that an animal had entered the house.

Diane came cautiously down the creaky staircase and we inspected the door together. There was no evidence anything had been thrown at the door, such as a log, brick, or some other kind of heavy object. There was nothing of note on the front porch outside the house, either. No clues. I inspected the grass on the sides of the front porch and found no evidence that someone had stepped on the grass anywhere around the porch. This confirmed my remembrance of the *BOOM!* For I had heard no sounds of a person running, breathing, laughing; nor did I feel the vibrations of someone running down the steps or jumping off the porch and hitting the ground in escape. The porch is four steps up from the ground; the impact of feet hitting the ground from that height sends a vibration wave right through the house. But there had been none.

All the windows in my bedroom were wide open at the time of the intrusion. The night had been hot and airless. I'm sure I would have heard something or felt the vibrations of a person running away from the damaged door after the offense—if a person was the cause of the intrusion. However, as Diane pointed out, there is a slight chance we may not have heard a person running away because I had the fan running in the bedroom while we were sleeping. The fan's "white noise" might have covered the intruder's noises, such as feet running away, and maybe the laughter of pranksters. I didn't think she was correct, but she had a point that had to be considered.

After ten minutes of inspection, and searching the dark yard and silent street with a powerful flashlight for signs of a person or persons who might have done this injustice to us, we closed the front door and locked it and sat on the couch wringing our hands, our eyes focused on the door, our imaginations running wild, at a complete loss as to who or what had caused this madness. We could not understand why anyone would want to try to break in a house at 3:45 a.m. when two cars were sitting in the driveway and it was obvious the occupants were at home. Moreover, since the intruder successfully got the front door open, why didn't he—or they—complete the mission and enter the house? After all, whoever it was who woke us up was willing to break the door in: why not follow up with a burglary and rob us? To me, that would be a sign of very poor planning if the intruders were indeed planning to rob us.

The surface of the door was dusty, but there were no handprints. There were no scratches on the door from the claws of a raccoon, opossum or cat, and the screen was not torn or scratched either. It had simply been pushed out of the way, out of the screen door, when the thing that caused the *BOOM!* banged right through it to pound the main door open. I had left the door unlocked, that's why the door flew open. If I had locked it, I suspect the door would have cracked. This occurred in a neighborhood where people are generally soundly asleep by 1 a.m. on a Saturday night.

After we ruled out the likelihood of a person causing the harm, and animals, such as a cat or a raccoon, trying to get in the house, we were left to consider the paranormal. In my head, I was already thinking out-of-space people were the culprits. Later in the day, when we were investigating Camp Hero in Montauk, I would tell my story to Nick Voulgaris, MUFON's Chief Investigator in New York State, who was along for the investigation, and he said, "Why would extraterrestrials have to break in? They would have been able to just go through the walls."

Of course, Nick was right.

There have been many cases of aliens moving right through solid objects without disturbing them. A case in point is the famous Brooklyn Bridge Abduction, which abduction researcher Budd Hopkins investigated and documented. This case is also known as the "Manhattan Abduction." It occurred at an apartment building next to the Brooklyn Bridge at three in the morning on November 30, 1989. A woman was reportedly transported right through the glass of a window in the wall of her apartment without the window breaking. The sleeping woman was brought into a spaceship hovering high over the building. Three beings she called "Greys" brought her to a huge spaceship where she was examined. The event was reportedly witnessed by two bodyguards for the former United Nations

Secretary General. Supposedly, Javier Perez de Cuellar was also present and witnessed the event.

At five in the morning, as dawn cracked in the tired eastern sky, Diane and I finally went back to bed. We slept lightly till the alarm clock went off at 10 a.m.

One thought I had about the event that terrified me was, what if the intruders actually did get in the house and did what they wanted to do to us but we just don't remember anything about it?

55

Camp Hero and the Montauk Project.

Sign at entrance to Camp Hero State Park with the Montauk Point Lighthouse in the background. What secrets are buried within?

We drove out to Camp Hero State Park at Montauk Point and arrived at the parking lot overlooking the craggy, brown dirt bluffs. The bluffs loom high over dangerous crashing waves of the Atlantic Ocean on rocks below. The time was two in the afternoon.

Montauk is the easternmost town on Long Island's south fork and is referred to by some people as The End, which was the name of a movie that was filmed in Montauk. The town is well established as a tourist haven. It has motels and miles of beaches, great dining, fun bars with music, and loads of opportunities for hiking and great bike riding.

The town is also the site where three girls found and photographed a dead animal on the beach in 2004 that became known as the Montauk Monster. Some people said it was a raccoon that had been floating in the ocean for some time and rotted in the saltwater and sun, creating the appearance of a small monster. A photo of the creature appeared on CNN a day or so after it was discovered, and stories about the Monster flared across the Internet.

Some years later, I spoke by telephone with the girl who photographed the animal on the beach. She was attending college in Hawaii when I reached her. She said she didn't know what happened to the body of the creature after she photographed it. Some people at the time claimed a government agent took off with the Montauk Monster. They said the monster was an alien. They claimed the government wanted to get rid of it before police and scientists could examine it.

Other people speculated that an examination of the dead animal that washed up on the beach could have revealed that the creature was a monster that had been created in an experiment that went out of control on Plum Island. Plum Island is a Homeland Security-controlled facility for animal disease study. It's located a mile off Long Island's east end. The facility is not accessible to the general public. The woman I spoke with said she and two friends who were with her when she photographed the beast now all shared the copyrights to the photo. She said she and her friends hired lawyers to sue people who published their photograph of the Montauk Monster without their permission. In several later e-mails I sent her, I offered her money to let me publish the photo she took of the supposed Montauk Monster, but she never responded.

For many years, Montauk has been associated with strange events, such as UFOs seen overhead and submerging into the ocean and emerging from it. Ghosts are also known to appear at various places, including the site where the Native Americans from Montauk had a battle with the Pequot tribe from Connecticut.

According to Preston Nichols, author of *The Montauk Project* (with Peter Moon), a UFO had been sucked into an underground location at Camp Hero as a result of experiments in time travel. Presumably, it is still there, but possibly buried in concrete that may have later been poured on top of it. Camp Hero was the very place Diane and I and our friends were investigating on this Sunday, the day following the night something broke into my house.

According to Nichols, there are also stories of strange events that took place in Montauk. These stories include days when many of the local wild animals in the woods left the trees and came into town for unknown reasons, possibly for protection. He claimed it had something to do with mood changes resulting from radio waves beamed from Camp Hero, as part of the secretive experiments that went on there for many years.

Camp Hero is a former Air Force base with a huge radar on top a building overlooking the Atlantic Ocean. The radar still sits atop this building. It's the place where the experiments in mind control allegedly took place up until 1983.

During World War II, the base had large guns to shoot at German spy boats, including submarines. During the war, German soldiers in U-boats studied

Casting an eerie gloom over Camp Hero State Park is a giant radar reflector set atop a building on grounds that are off limits to the public. What took place inside the building? Were experiments in time travel and mind control really conducted there for many years without official government sanction?

American military movement along New York's coastline from the ocean. The Germans were very good at spying on the United States from the ocean. In fact, a German submarine successfully landed men on a beach in nearby Amagansett at the height of the war, but the German agents were found out early and were arrested before they could do any damage to the United States.

When Camp Hero's radar technology was surpassed by superior satellite technology, the radar was rendered obsolete and the base was shut down in 1969. The property was transferred to the New York State Office of Parks, Recreation, and Historic Preservation in the 1980s, and thus became a state park for residents to enjoy. It was during the years between 1970 and 1983 that the former base was used for experiments, Nichols claims.

The park is located right next to the famous Montauk Point Lighthouse. It is reached by driving on the same road that enters Montauk State Park. A big sign announces Camp Hero State Park. A fee is required to enter the park during the summer season. Vehicles must stop at a little booth at the park's entrance to pay. Various buildings on the grounds give testimony to its former military days. All the buildings are closed and derelict. Many people I have spoken with feel a palpable eeriness at the park. They say it hangs in the air, as if the place is haunted.

We were assembling at Camp Hero on this sunny day to discuss the Montauk Project. Camp Hero is the site where the alleged secretive experiments known as the Montauk Project took place. The experiments, and preparations to the facility to house the experiments, spanned thirteen years after the base was officially decommissioned by the military. According to Nichols, the experiments were largely funded by $10 billion in Nazi gold that was confiscated during World War II. The scientists leading the experiments were supposedly from private companies in conjunction with secretive military and government agents. They were part of a subterranean military industrial complex that sought to gain from the experimentation. Nichols indicates experimentation was greatly aided by technology gotten from alien civilizations, including the Sirians and Orions, respectively from the star systems Sirius and Orion.

Congress and the public were not aware of the experiments, Nichols tells us. A United States senator who got wind of the project, and investigated funding for it, could find no evidence of any United States involvement in the projects at Camp Hero. Nichols included copies of papers he said he found strewn around Camp Hero's facilities that indicate daily activities taking place there during years when nothing was supposedly going on at the abandoned former Air Force base.

The Montauk Project is the umbrella name Nichols gave for projects involving experiments in brain washing, mind control, time travel, and forms of dematerialization and materialization that occurred outside the government's official knowledge. According to Nichols, he was directly involved in a key aspect of the experiments, which concluded in 1983.

Most disturbing is that children had been used in the experiments, Nichols wrote. The book alleges that children and adults who participated in the experiments were lost in future time, in the year 6037 in a dead zone where nothing moved, like in a dream, never to return. He said thousands of people were abandoned in the future.

A monster was also created from out of the ether. A Bigfoot-like monster came into our world from some other dimension and reeked havoc at Camp Hero before it was sent back to the dimension from which it came. The book shows a photo of a black form that is identified as a "phantom phenomenon" that was photographed in an underground bunker in 1986, years after the experiments concluded. This leads us to believe the big black creature might still be present at the site, though Nichols does not specifically say that is the case.

Nichols said the radar tower that still exists and sits on the most prominent building at Camp Hero was used in conjunction with a "seat" that was created by renown inventor Nikola Tesla. Psychics would sit in the seat to go into other time periods and into other realities using their developed psychic abilities and the Montauk Project's advanced alien-inspired technology. Nichols reminds us that Tesla claimed to have communicated with aliens. Critics of Tesla's claim, however, that the communication through radio waves that Tesla believed he had with aliens was actually a natural phenomenon of clicking of electromagnetic energy and not aliens sending messages.

But endlessly fascinating to me, and worth repeating in this discussion, is the possibility that the government has been using technology and ideas given to them by aliens from Sirius and Orion. If this is true, how did such interaction come about?

Is our government in constant communication with alien beings? Is this the reason why the United States government has been so secretive and evasive about whether or not it has made contact with aliens? Or is our government afraid of the aliens? Is it working on devising ways to fight them on our behalf? Either way, there's got to be a reason why our government does not inform us as to their contact with aliens. I suspect they do not tell us what they know because the public would panic if we knew too much. We have to believe the government has good reason for what it does. We better hope so.

The Montauk Project experiments tie into the Philadelphia Experiment. That experiment was allegedly conducted in 1943. In it, the government tried to make the USS *Eldridge* invisible in Philadelphia Harbor by encapsulating it in a "bottle" of electromagnetic distortion to radars, rendering it invisible to the enemy. However, according to Nichols, the experiment rendered the ship actually invisible, killing men as it was magically teleported to Norfolk, Virginia, then back to Philadelphia.

Those men who did not die by becoming part of the USS *Eldridge's* molecular fabric—face half-in and half-out of the metal bulkhead—went crazy, mostly as a result of having been sent into some kind of ungodly oblivion before they returned.

We listened to Peggy Vetrano of ESP, who led the investigation at Camp Hero, explain what the Montauk Project was, and what it might mean to humanity if it actually took place.

At one point, later in the day, after a lengthy and largely unproductive EVP session involving two versions of the Ovilus (versions 1 and 3) Peggy said, "When are we going to get down to it? When are we going to get deeper?" She lifted up her hands and shook them like a white Voodoo priestess: "I don't mean, 'I think

I heard a ghost.' I mean really getting down inside of things to understand them?"

Peggy seemed frustrated by the inability of the paranormal to extend itself to us, making the Unknown forever inaccessible, it seemed. This included accessing the truth of what actually took place at Camp Hero.

I have often felt the same frustration. The nature of the paranormal is inexplicable, even illogical. Sometimes it seems you can only get so far and that's as far as you'll ever be able to go. We would most likely never know the truth of what took place at Camp Hero, or of what the government knows about aliens. And we'll probably never know what the aliens are up to on our planet.

Paranormal Researcher Peggy Vetrano of Eastern Suffolk Paranormal leads a group of investigators at Camp Hero State Park at Montauk Point. This is the site of the alleged Montauk Project. The radar in the background was reportedly instrumental in mind control experiments,

I wrote to Preston Nichols a year before this trip and tried to get him to join Peggy, Diane, me, and others to give us a tour of Camp Hero and explain what took place in each area and what he remembered doing there. But he never responded.

After assembling at the parking lot of Camp Hero State Park, the ten of us who attended the day's adventure drove to the radar tower where Peggy led the discussion of what took place in the tower building connected to the Montauk Project. She discussed the "seat" where psychics sat and were transported to some other place thousands of years into the future where a gold horse stood in the center of a square and offered knowledge to those who teleported there.

There was so much for us to discuss at this place. We found large concrete manhole covers that we believe opened to the same tunnels where the "phantom phenomenon" was photographed and may still dwell, for all we know.

While it was all fascinating, my mind was stuck on the UFO that was reportedly buried at the site. So I went back to the book itself, *The Montauk Project*, to see what Preston Nichols said about the UFO. He said it had a technology that humans wanted. It involved a crystal. He said the aliens didn't want us to have it. He indicated that cement trucks were seen entering Camp Hero after the experiments concluded. The underground area where the UFO is located might have been filled in with cement. So it might never be found again. Just another layer of frustration added to efforts in accessing knowledge.

PART VI

CONCLUSION

56

When?

So, now, dear reader, I have introduced myself to you and told you all about the silent alien invasion of Long Island. I have done my job as a reporter. But my work has only started. My investigation must continue. Sometimes I find myself smiling when my thoughts replay the words Peggy Vetrano spoke at Camp Hero about not being able to readily access the paranormal and the Unknown. I wonder all the time when we humans will we ever "get down to it" and really understand what's going on in this crazy inaccessible universe with so many mysteries piled on top of so many secrets piled on top of so much our minds can not grasp. When will we be able to see with any clarity?

When?

The summer is over. It was a weird one, for sure.

Tonight, a cold November wind bears down on Long Island. Winter is coming. Earlier, during the day, the sky was dark and brooding. It dropped a little rain. Large bruised clouds moved slowly overhead as a howl in the wind carried across the Pine Barrens like crying wraiths. I stood among the trees watching their limbs twist and sing as they rubbed against one another like spiky octopus tentacles. UFOs are interested in the Pine Barrens, so in a round about way, I'm back where I started as a reporter in 1989, writing about Long Island's primal forest. Funny how things work—how everything is connected to the next thing. I'm still learning about all that. It brings me back to Peggy's question: "When?"

Accepting our limitations as humans—enough to soak in the changes the universe has thrown at us, and noticing as a species that we are being visited by other species from the sky—will take some getting used to. "There are tongues in the trees, books in the brooks..." Maybe Shakespeare's optimism is too hopeful.

It's a wait-and-see situation. Not many possible outcomes, however. It will probably end badly for us.

I sit here tonight wrapped in a thick, old blanket in a beach chair low to the ground at the back of Almshouse Cemetery in Yaphank. It's about midnight. My flashlight is pointed at the notebook I am always carrying, writing these words. It's the place where all this started for me with a CE-5 meditation.

I am here tonight, alone, to call the aliens down once again: just me and them this time. It's probably true that once a reporter, always a reporter: Tonight I will put my experiences with flying saucers to the test and seek to meet extraterrestrials face-to-face to record their messages. What is there to lose at this point? All there is are questions. My time is spent running across Long Island in search of answers, but my heart already knows the only answers to be found will probably be gotten right here, from somewhere above the trees: just me and them, face-to-face in old Potter's Field. So be it.

To that end, as of the time of this writing, I have plans to sign on as a MUFON field investigator. It's a noble goal for me to accomplish sometime in early 2014. That will make me one of only a handful of MUFON field investigators on all of Long Island. We will need more, many more. We must go deeper into the study of UFOs. Where are flying saucers hiding? What are the aliens' weaknesses? We must make contact, and soon. If what experts are saying is right, there's not much time left before the great introduction of the space visitors to Humankind: the Great Coming. Peggy Vetrano's words stay in my head and ring like bells. "When will we get down to it?" My focus must be to split the question "When?" right down the middle and enter head first to look inside and find the answers we all seek. I'm a reporter, after all. That's my job.

Ending this book and saying goodbye to you is a departure point in my life. Maybe my questions and the answers to be received, if any, will seal me into a place that will be like the dead zone where the Montauk Experiment victims are stuck, in a place where nothing moves, and only the gold horse in the square has the answers. My job will be riding the gold horse.

I need some sleep, been up continuously for too many hours. I close my eyes now against the cold night for awhile. The wind burns my face. Thank you for being with me up to now, dear reader. From here, my journey will be traveled alone. My goal will be to seek the truth as to the extent of the alien invasion as best as it can be found. My guess is you would have to call me a "resister" or a member of the alien "Resistance." There have to be others out there like me. Maybe you'll be one soon, too, if you're not one already. Our hope should be that the government is on our side, protecting us from our enemies in the sky. We must believe and have confidence that agents from the Anti-UFO Army are working to free us from the alien grip. I'm ready for what may come. I suspect it will be War.

*

My gaze is now cast in the direction of Southaven Park. It is located five miles northeast through the midnight forest. The wind is really wild and brittle cold now.

My eyes are closed, relaxed against the biting night. A hush falls over me. Soon self-hypnosis techniques come to mind to relax my body and brain.

In my mind, a wave of warm light overtakes my body, relaxing me as the light creeps its way up from my toes to the top of my head. Count backwards starting at 10, and go all the way down to zero. Take your time. Each number appears in my thoughts in the form of a fluffy, white cloud that dissipates against a blue sky the color of a robin's egg as it is slowly replaced by another puffy number, counting down, down, down to zero.

Then in my mind my body leaves Earth, just as Dr. Greer had instructed in his meditation for CE-5 enthusiasts to do to reach the aliens. Soon leaving the solar system and entering deep dark space with a hundred billion stars all around. It's beautiful.

Earth is now behind me. My body floats like an astronaut's without a spacesuit. Peggy Vetrano's words are keeping me company. They float in space beside me. My inner voice calls upon any and all aliens to hear my words: "Come to me. Visit me on Earth. Go where my mind shows you., Follow my thoughts." Repeat this message several times along with other things such as, "Come in peace. Don't hurt me." Sometimes the question "When?" slips into my thoughts, but I don't mean for it to. I'm mixing dreams with hypnosis. The words float around me: "…get down to it…When?"

My thoughts turn around so my body is facing Earth: "Follow me," my telepathic thoughts tell the space creatures who I do not see anywhere. The Earth is blue and white and green and brown and gorgeous. Then the solar system fades away and my body falls to Earth, right into the haunted graveyard where my form sits alone in the cold wind under a dark night sky. My thoughts are dreamy: "When?"

My eyes open to a sudden bright light above. My sense is a lot of time has passed. But where did it go? Fell asleep? Though I am scared stiff and breathless as I observe the miracle, the curse, I can't help but smile. My mind races with questions, the answers to some of which are in front of me right now. What will happen next? My body is shivering. Where will all this bring me? Stay alert and observant. Will I be given knowledge? Will it help Humanity fight the aliens?

When?

When?

-30-

BIBLIOGRAPHY

"An Aerial Mystery," *New York Times*, September 12, 1880.

Dennett, Preston. *UFOs Over New York: A True History of Extraterrestrial Encounters in the Empire State.* (Atglen, PA: Schiffer Publishing, Ltd., 2008).

Flammer, Joseph, and Diane Hill. *Ghosts, Ghouls, and Monsters of Long Island.* (Atglen, PA: Schiffer Publishing, Ltd., 2012).

Foxnews.com. "Investigators want missile theory probed in '96 TWA Flight 800 crash," June 19, 2013. http://www.foxnews.com/us/.

Kean, Leslie. *UFOs: Generals, Pilots, And Government Officials Go On The Record.* (New York, New York: Three Rivers Press, 2010).

Keel, John, A. The Mothman Prophecies. (New York, NY: Tom Doherty Associates, 1975).

Kitei, Lynne, D., MD, *The Phoenix Lights: A Skeptic's Discovery That We Are Not Alone.* (Charlottesville, VA: Hampton Roads Publishing Company, Inc., 2004).

Nichols, Preston, B. (with Peter Moon). *The Montauk Project: Experiments In Time.* (Westbury, NY: Sky Books, 1992).

Randle, Kevin, D., *Crash: When UFOs Fall From the Sky.* (Franklin Lakes, NJ: New Page Books, 2010).

Romanek, Stan (with J. Allan Danelek). *Messages: The World's Most Documented Extraterrestrial Contact Story.* (Woodbury, Minnesota: Llewellyn Publications, 2009).

UFOCasebook.com. "The Manhattan Abduction" (Linda Cortile Napolitano), http://www.ufocasebook.com/Manhattan.html.

"UFO Crash at Southaven Park, 1992." *South Shore Press:* Volume No. 7: May 25, 1993.

INDEX